SIMPLY DIGITAL PHOTOGRAPHY

by Rob Sheppard

WILEY

A John Wiley and Sons, Ltd, Publication

First published under the title Digital Photography Simplified by **Wiley Publishing, Inc.** 10475 Crosspoint Boulevard Indianapolis, IN 46256, USA

This edition first published 2010.

Registered office

John Wiley & Sons Ltd, The Atrium, Southern Gate, Chichester, West Sussex, PO19 8SQ, United Kingdom

For details of our global editorial offices, for customer services and for information about how to apply for permission to reuse the copyright material in this book please see our website at www.wiley.com.

Wiley also publishes its books in a variety of electronic formats. Some content that appears in print may not be available in electronic books.

ISBN: 978-0-470-71132-3

A catalogue record for this book is available from the British Library.

Printed in Italy by Printer Trento

Publisher's Acknowledgements

Some of the people who helped bring this book to market include the following:

Editorial and Production

VP Consumer and Technology Publishing Director: Michelle Leete

Associate Director – Book Content Management: Martin Tribe

Associate Publisher: Chris Webb

Executive Commissioning Editor: Birgit Gruber

Publishing Assistant: Ellie Scott

Project Editor: Juliet Booker

Development Editor: Shena Deuchars

Marketing

Senior Marketing Manager: Louise Breinholt

Marketing Executives: Chloe Tunnicliffe and Kate Parrett

Composition Services

Layout: Andrea Hornberger, Jennifer Mayberry

Graphics: Jill A. Proll

Indexer: Potomac Indexing, LLC

Series Designer: Patrick Cunningham

About the Author

Rob Sheppard is the author and photographer of more than 25 books, a well-known speaker and workshop leader, and editor-at-large and columnist for the prestigious *Outdoor Photographer* magazine. As an author and photographer, Sheppard has written hundreds of articles about photography and nature, plus books ranging from guides to photography such as *Digital Photography: Top 100 Simplified Tips & Tricks*, to books about Photoshop including *Adobe Camera Raw for Digital Photographers Only* and *Outdoor Photographer Landscape and Nature Photography with Photoshop CS2*. His website is at www.robsheppardphoto.com and his blog is at www.photodigitary.com.

Author's Acknowledgements

Any book is only possible with the help of a lot of people. I thank all the folks at Wiley for their work in creating books like this and their work in helping make the book the best it can be. I really appreciate all the work that editor Sarah Hellert did, along with her associates, in helping keep this book clear and understandable for the reader. I also thank my terrific wife of 28 years who keeps me grounded and focused while I work on my books. I thank the people at Werner Publications, my old home, where I was editor of *Outdoor Photographer* for 12 years and helped start *PC Photo* magazine — I thank them for their continued support so I can stay on top of changes in the industry. I especially thank Chris Robinson, Wes Pitts, and Steve Werner for their efforts in keeping a strong magazine presence in the photo market, and a place for my work, too. That magazine work enhances and enriches what I can do for readers of my books. And I thank Rick Sammon for his support and inspiration in doing photography books.

How to Use This Book

Do you look at the pictures in a book before anything else on a page? Would you rather see an image instead of read about how to do something? Search no further. This book is for you. Opening *SIMPLY Digital Photography* allows you to read less and learn more about digital photography.

Who Needs This Book

This book is for a reader who has limited experience with a digital camera or a photo editing program and wants to learn more. It is also for readers who want to expand or refresh their knowledge of the different aspects of digital photography.

What You Need to Use This Book

- A digital camera

To install and run Photoshop Elements, you need a computer with the following:

- Windows: An Intel Pentium 4, Celeron, or compatible processor at 1.3 GHz or faster;
  Mac: PowerPC G4 or G5 or multicore Intel processor
- Windows XP with Service Pack 2 or Windows Vista operating system; Mac OS X v10.4.8 and up
- Colour monitor with a minimum of 1024 × 768 resolution (a 19-inch monitor is recommended)
- 256 MB of RAM (1 GB recommended)
- 1.5 GB of available hard-disk space (10 to 20 GB free space is recommended)
- CD-ROM or DVD-ROM drive

The Conventions in This Book

A number of typographic and layout styles have been used throughout *SIMPLY Digital Photography* to distinguish different types of information.

Bold

Bold type represents the names of commands and options that you interact with. Bold type also indicates text and numbers that you must type into a dialog box.

Italics

Italic words introduce a new term, which is then defined.

Numbered Steps

You must perform the instructions in numbered steps in order to successfully complete a section and achieve the final results.

Bulleted Steps

These steps point out various optional features. You do not have to perform these steps; they simply give additional information about a feature.

Notes

Notes give additional information. They may describe special conditions that may occur during an operation. They may warn you of a situation that you want to avoid – for example, the loss of data. A note may also cross-reference a related area of the book. A cross-reference may guide you to another chapter or to another section within the current chapter.

Icons and Buttons

Icons and buttons are graphical representations within the text. They show you exactly what you need to click to perform a step.

You can easily identify the tips in any section by looking for the tip icon. Tips offer additional information, including hints, warnings and tricks. You can use the tip information to go beyond what you have learned in the steps.

Operating System Differences

The screenshots used in this book were captured using the Windows Vista operating system. The features shown in the tasks may differ slightly if you are using Windows 7, Windows XP or an earlier operating system. For example, the default folder for saving photos in Windows Vista is named "Pictures," whereas the default folder in Windows XP for saving photos is named "My Pictures." The program workspace may also look different based on your monitor resolution setting and your program preferences.

Table of Contents

3 USING LIGHT TO YOUR ADVANTAGE — 38

4 UNDERSTANDING EXPOSURE AND WHITE BALANCE — 60

5 CHOOSING SHUTTER SPEED AND F-STOP — 78

6 GETTING MAXIMUM SHARPNESS — 92

9 EDITING AND ORGANISING YOUR PHOTOS 138

10 BASIC ADJUSTMENTS WITH PHOTOSHOP ELEMENTS 154

CONTENTS

GETTING READY TO TAKE PICTURES

No matter what camera you have, you can customise it so that it works really well for you. Camera manufacturers make a lot of decisions about how a camera works based on what they think photographers who might buy a particular camera will need or use.

However, manufacturers can only guess, and sometimes, the default settings of your camera are designed for the needs of the average photographer; as a result, they are not optimal for a person who wants to take better photographs.

Is your camera set up right to support your picture taking? In this chapter, you learn the basics of getting ready to take great pictures with your camera.

SET UP YOUR LCD FOR OPTIMUM USE

The LCD on a digital camera is a wonderful invention. It gives you an accurate view of your subject so that you see exactly what you are going to get in your photograph. But in order to get the most from your LCD, you need to use the camera's menus to make some choices about how it works. You want to be sure it is helping you, not holding you back. Here are some tips in setting up your camera for the best use of your LCD.

Review Time

After you take the picture, the actual image shows up on most LCDs. This image review gives you a quick look at what your photo looks like. For example, you can quickly look to see that it is sharp and that your subject's eyes are open. You know immediately if you need to make changes to your photography.

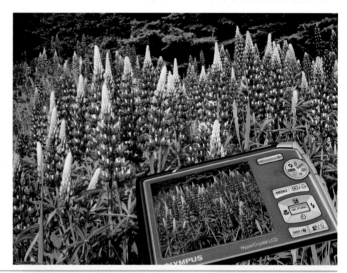

Set Review Time

On most cameras you can set review time between about 2 and 10 seconds in the camera or setup menus. Short times are not of much value because you really cannot evaluate much of what is in the picture. Try 8 to 10 seconds. Once you have seen enough, press the shutter release lightly and the review goes away. If the time is too short, simply press your playback button for a longer view.

Auto Rotate

Most digital cameras today automatically rotate a vertical picture so that it shows up vertically in the LCD when you hold the camera horizontally. Unfortunately, a vertical picture does not fill the horizontal space and uses the LCD inefficiently. You can get the most from your LCD and get the largest picture possible if you set the camera so that it does not auto-rotate vertical pictures. The Auto Rotate setting is usually in the playback or setup menus.

Camera Sleep Time (Auto Power Down)

A frustrating thing for digital photographers is to try to take a picture and find that your camera has gone to sleep. Most digital cameras have the auto power down time set too early. This option is usually in the setup menu and a good setting would be 2 to 4 minutes for most people. You can set this time longer but then you could be using your battery more than you want to.

VIEWFINDER OR LCD – WHICH TO USE?

Many cameras have both a viewfinder and an LCD. Viewfinders can be either optical or electronic (known as "EVF"). A viewfinder only works when you hold your eye up to it. Most people use the LCD when possible because it seems so natural to do. And some cameras do not even have viewfinders. Why would you want to use a viewfinder rather than an LCD? There are some distinct advantages to both. Knowing the possibilities of a viewfinder can help you use your camera better.

Use the Viewfinder in Bright Light

LCDs can be hard to see in bright light, especially when there are bright subjects that you are photographing. Because an optical or electronic viewfinder limits extraneous light and your head blocks more light, both allow you to see the subject better for framing in those conditions.

Use the LCD Inside

The LCD is ideal for shooting indoors. It has a consistent brightness, even if the light is low, which makes it easier to use than a viewfinder in those conditions. It also shows you if your exposure and white balance are correct so that you can get the best-looking image.

Use the Viewfinder for Moving Subjects

Movement can be hard to follow with an LCD held away from your face. This is where a viewfinder comes in handy. You have to have the camera up to your eyes to use a viewfinder. This makes it easier to follow movement (the camera simply follows your gaze) and distracting movement around the camera and LCD is blocked from view and not seen. Optical viewfinders are especially good for action.

Use the LCD for Close Shooting

Your LCD is showing you exactly what the lens is seeing on your camera. A separate optical viewfinder, as used on compact digital cameras has its own lens system, and so it is seeing something slightly different. At a distance, this does not matter. But when you get up close, the optical viewfinder may not frame the scene correctly, which can mean that parts of your subject get cut off. You never have that problem with the LCD.

CHOOSE A RESOLUTION AND FILE TYPE

Your camera comes with a certain resolution, such as 10 or 12 megapixels. This resolution strongly affects the price of your camera and the capabilities of the sensor. Your camera also comes with a default setting for the file type and compression that may or may not be best for you. Understanding a little about resolution and image files will ensure that you make the right choices for the highest-quality photos. This will also mean you get your money's worth from your camera and sensor.

Find Your Settings

Resolution and file type are settings that affect image size and quality. They are usually found in the camera operation section of the menus for your camera. Unfortunately, camera manufacturers have not made the icons for these settings consistent so you may have to check your manual.

Use Your Megapixels

A common way of showing image size is L, M, and S (for large, medium, and small resolution). Large uses the full size of your camera's sensor, giving you the megapixels you paid for. Use it. Only use the smaller sizes if you really have to get small photos, such as for a Web site, and you are sure that you will never need a large photo.

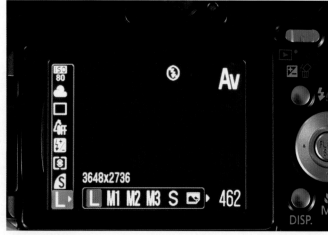

Choose JPEG with High Quality

The default image type for most digital cameras is JPEG shot at medium compression or *quality* (quality refers to how the image is compressed for size). For optimum JPEG images, choose the highest-quality compression, such as Superfine. This makes files a little larger, but not much, and so you might need a slightly larger memory card to handle the file sizes.

What About RAW?

Some compact digital cameras and all digital SLRs include an image type called RAW. This is a special format that saves far more tonal and colour information from the sensor than JPEG offers. It is very useful for photographers who want to do extensive processing on their images in the computer. It does not have more detail than a JPEG file (that is dependent on megapixels).

CHOOSE A MEMORY CARD

Your camera is built to hold a certain type of memory card. A memory card stores your pictures and you save photos to it or erase photos from it. These cards come in a variety of types such as CompactFlash or SD cards, but your camera is only designed for one type (except for a few digital SLRs that have slots for two). While you cannot decide what type to use, you do need to decide how large a card to get and whether speed will affect this choice.

Memory Card Types

You should know your memory card type so that you can recognise it in a store and be sure you have the right type. Each card type is quite different in size and shape. Open the door to the memory card slot on your camera and take out the memory card to see exactly what it looks like (be sure the camera is off when you do this).

Choose Memory Capacity

Memory cards have become less expensive for more capacity. It is easy to find 1 or 2 GB cards at very affordable prices. The larger the capacity, the greater the number of images you can store. Capacity is key with higher-megapixel cameras and especially for RAW files. A 2 GB card is a good starting size and will hold about 500 standard quality, full-resolution JPEGs from a 10-megapixel camera.

How Important Is Memory Card Speed?

You will often see memory cards listed with speeds – 80X, 100X, and higher. This does not speed up your camera. It affects how fast images are recorded to the memory card from the camera's memory buffer. Keep in mind that not all cameras support high speeds. Speed can also affect how fast you can download images to your computer.

Download from a Memory Card

A simple way of downloading photos is to use your camera and the cable that came with it. A better way is to get a memory card reader. A memory card reader is usually faster, takes up little space on your desk or computer and never has problems with battery power (if your camera loses power while downloading, you can lose your photos).

HOLD THE CAMERA FOR SHARPNESS

Digital cameras are capable of truly excellent sharpness. Yet all too often photographers are disappointed by blurry photos. They look unsharp, and people often blame "cheap cameras." Yet, the number one cause of blurriness is camera movement during exposure. How you hold the camera and release the shutter can determine whether you capture a sharp or blurry photo. This will be especially noticeable if you want to enlarge the image in a big print.

Camera Movement Causes Blurry Photos

When a camera is handheld, it can move slightly while taking the picture. As shutter speeds get slower, this means blur in your photo and sharpness that is much less than your camera is capable of. Even if the blur is not obvious, it can still be there, degrading the contrast of the image. No amount of work on the computer can make these images truly sharp.

Support the Camera Well

Support your camera to minimise camera movement. With a digital SLR, put your left hand, palm up, under the lens, with your right hand gripping the side securely. With compact cameras, keep both hands gripping the sides solidly (no one-handed shooting!). Then keep your elbows in to the side of your chest as you photograph, in order to keep arm movement to a minimum.

Squeeze the Shutter

Holding the camera securely does not help if you punch the shutter button. Put your finger on the shutter button and then squeeze your finger down in a smooth motion to push the button and take a picture. Keep your finger depressed as the shutter goes off and then release it gently.

Turn Your Car Off for Sharpness

Go to any national park and you will see people driving along, photographing from cars, bracing their arms against the frame of an open window. A moving car, combined with the vibration from the motor, always causes problems with camera movement and blurry photos. For optimum sharpness, stop the car and turn off the engine for the picture. At a minimum, avoid leaning against the car frame if the car is running.

CHOOSE A PROGRAM MODE

Digital cameras typically have a choice of several modes of operation that affect exposure and how an image is captured. These programmed ways of operating the camera offer you options that affect how you can get the best pictures of a particular subject or scene. They are often set up for specific subjects or types of scene so that the camera can be quickly prepared for them. By understanding a bit about them, you can quickly choose what works best for you.

Exposure Mode Choices

Cameras have to be set for a proper exposure. That includes both a shutter speed, which affects action, and an aperture or f-stop, which affects depth of field (sharpness in depth). These settings also affect how much light comes through the camera. Exposure modes change how these controls are chosen – that is, how much is done by the camera's internal electronics and how much you control.

Program, Aperture-Priority, and Shutter Speed-Priority

All digital SLRs and many small digital cameras include the modes P for Program, A or Av for Aperture-Priority, and S or Tv for Shutter Speed-Priority exposure. The camera chooses both shutter speed and aperture in P, making it good for quick shots. In A, you choose an aperture for depth-of-field and the camera sets the shutter speed. In S, you choose a shutter speed and the camera sets the appropriate aperture or f-stop.

Program Modes

Many popular cameras include special program modes that are designed to make decisions easier about setting up a camera for specific subjects. You will find options such as Landscape, which affects exposure, colour, ISO setting, and white balance for scenic pictures; Portrait, which affects the same things for close-up shots of people; and Sports, which is designed to optimise the camera for action.

Do You Need Manual Mode?

Manual is a mode where you set all exposure parameters yourself. Many photographers never need it but it is helpful when conditions seem to fool all the other modes. In Manual mode, you can set shutter speed and f-stop based on how the meter works in your camera, take a picture, and then check your exposure in the LCD. If the exposure is not what you need from a scene, you can then change the shutter speed or f-stop until it is right.

USE YOUR CAMERA'S AUTOFOCUS

Autofocus, or AF, is a great innovation. The camera works with the lens to determine where the lens needs to focus. AF helps your camera and lens find the right things to make sharp in your scene. That makes it easy to photograph something quickly, but AF can focus in the wrong places. However, you can learn how to control it. A few simple techniques will help you ensure that the autofocus is finding the right part of your scene to focus on.

Focus Points Are Important

One of the most annoying things for a photographer is to have a nice picture where the focus is in the wrong place. For example, you have a great shot of grandma but she is not sharp, though the tree behind her is. Or your beautiful flower stays blurred while the woodchip mulch behind it is sharp. Learn to look quickly at a scene so that you know which are the most important points that must be sharp.

Lock Focus on Your Subject

Once you know what has to be sharp, point your camera, set it on single-shot AF at that point and then press your shutter button slightly to lock focus. The camera usually beeps or gives some other indicator of focus. While still pressing the shutter button, quickly move the camera to frame your shot properly and then take the picture. Some cameras also have separate focus lock buttons.

Use Continuous Autofocus for Action

If you are photographing a sporting event such as a kids' football game, you usually cannot lock focus because of the continuous movement. Change your camera to continuous AF if it has that option. Now the camera continuously focuses as you shoot the action. Sometimes the action will be too fast for it to keep up but mostly it will keep finding the right focus as the action progresses.

Start Autofocus Early

Any AF system needs some time, however brief, to examine the scene, determine the focus point, and focus the lens. If you wait until you need that focus, especially with a moving subject, then you will often miss the shot because of this time delay. Start your autofocus early, before you need it, by lightly pressing your shutter button enough to get AF going, but not enough to trip the shutter.

CONTENTS

2

TAKING A BETTER PICTURE THROUGH COMPOSITION

Better photos start with *composition* – the way you arrange the subject, background, and other parts of a photograph within the image area. Sometimes this is referred to as "framing" the subject or scene. Any composition is based on your decisions on what to include in the photograph, what to keep out, and how to place your subject in the scene.

What makes a composition work? This chapter answers these questions, by showing you how to get better compositions in your photographs. You learn about some specific techniques that you can use with your camera and on your subjects.

SIMPLE PICTURES WORK BEST

A general tendency for beginning photographers is to try to get everything into one photograph. Instead of one goal for one photograph, they try to satisfy many goals in a single image. This can lead to busy, confusing photos that are not very satisfying to the photographer or a viewer of the image. By looking to make photographs simple and direct and by more clearly knowing what you want from a photo, you will quickly create more appealing photos.

Decide What Your Subject Really Is

Does this seem like an obvious point? Although it is important, too many photographers do not really consider it. You need to know what your subject really is so that you can be sure your composition is based around it. You may also run into trouble if you include multiple subjects in a photograph, as this will confuse your viewer.

Make Your Subject the Star

A composition that does not make the subject the star of the photograph is almost always a confusing image. Your subject should never be a secondary part of a photo. If you are photographing a person, for example, photograph that person, not the person and the rest of the world around them. Do not try to include too much.

Watch Out for Distractions

Distractions take the viewer's eye away from your subject. Keep them out of your photograph. Avoid really bright spots in the background, especially high in the picture, as they always attract the viewer's eye. Watch out for signs – your viewers will always try to read them. Be careful of high-contrast details that appear away from your subject, as they will draw the eye from your subject.

Use Your LCD Review

That LCD on the back of your camera is such a wonderful tool. It really helps with composition. Think of it as a little photograph. Do you like that photograph? Is the subject the star of that photograph? Are there distractions in the image area that are taking your eye away from the subject? Review your shot and be sure you got something that clearly favours the subject.

GET CLOSE TO YOUR SUBJECT

Your subject should be the star of your photos and one way to make that happen is to be sure you are close enough to the subject that it appears at a good size in your viewfinder. All too often, photographers step back from their subjects to get everything in, when they should, in fact, be stepping closer to get the best shot possible of that subject. Occasionally, it looks good to have a small subject with a huge scene, but most of the time, a large subject in the frame looks best.

Watch the Space Around Your Subject

Photographers often focus so hard on the subject that they do not really see the rest of the photograph. A way to force yourself to see the whole image is to look at the space around your subject when you review the shot in the LCD. That tells you a lot about space and subjects and helps you refine your shot.

Take a Step Closer

A great technique to try is to frame up your photo to get what you think is a good shot and then take a step closer while keeping the zoom untouched. Frame up and take the picture. That extra step often makes a more dynamic, interesting photo. It also forces you to deal with the subject differently within the image frame.

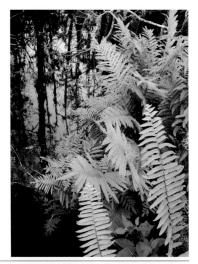

More Is Not Always Better

As noted in the last section, confusion as to what is really your subject can cause problems with your composition. This confusion often comes when photographers try to include more and more in their image. It is possible to create an interesting image with a lot of details, but it is a lot easier to create a strong photo by simplifying what you include in your photograph.

Experiment with Your Zoom

A great way of encouraging you to make a photo simple and direct is to challenge yourself with this exercise. Set your zoom to its strongest telephoto position. Then go out and take ten straight photos at that zoom position, never changing it to make a wider shot. This will make your photos look like you are close to your subject, even if you are not.

FIND A FOREGROUND

The foreground of your photo can make the difference between success and failure for a picture. The foreground is simply the area in front of your subject that is seen by your camera. Often photographers simply focus so much on the subject that they do not even see the problems and challenges of the foreground. Foregrounds can complement a subject or they can distract and detract from it. You always have the choice.

Use the Foreground for Depth

When you have a strong foreground to your photo, the image looks deeper. A photograph is a flat, two-dimensional object that tries to reflect a three-dimensional world. A good foreground creates and defines a relationship from close to far so that your composition has a feeling of three dimensions.

Look for a Frame

A quick and easy way of using your foreground is to look for a frame that will control what the viewer sees of the subject and background. This can be as simple as an interesting tree branch across the top of the photo. Or it can be an opening in a building or a rock formation that gives a view of your subject.

Get Close and Shoot through a Foreground

You cannot always get a foreground that is sharp. You can use that challenge as an opportunity for a better photo. Get up close to the foreground and shoot through it, almost like you would shoot through a frame, but use a telephoto setting on your zoom to make the foreground soft and not sharp.

Use a Wide-Angle View and Tilt Down

Often, photographers shoot a scene with a wide-angle lens to get it all in and then put the horizon right in the middle of the picture. Try, instead, to tilt the camera down so that you see the foreground better and then move to find something interesting in the foreground that you can include in your photo.

WATCH YOUR BACKGROUND

Just like the foreground, the background can make or break a picture. Often, photographers pay so much attention to the subject itself that they do not really see what is happening behind the subject. This is especially a problem with a digital SLR because the background often looks out of focus when you look through the lens and changes with the actual taking of the picture. But this happens with any camera when the photographer sees only the subject.

Distracting Backgrounds Hurt Your Subject

A constant challenge that photographers face is avoiding backgrounds that distract from or fight with their subject. Watch what is happening in a background and move your camera position to avoid things such as "hot spots" of light or bright colours.

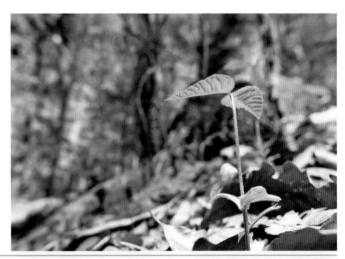

Simplify a Background

A great way to keep a background subordinate to your subject is to find an angle to your subject that keeps the background behind it simple. It is hard for a simple background to distract from your subject. Without a lot of stuff behind your subject, the viewer of your picture will see your subject more clearly.

Contrast Your Subject with the Background

Another way to ensure that your subject stands out is to look for contrast between it and the background. For example, if your subject is dark, see if you can get something light behind it or find a colour that is distinctly different from your subject.

Place Your Background

Even if you cannot get close to your subject, you can often make it stand out by placing your background carefully behind it. Find a bright spot and move so that the subject is in front of it. Or find a strong colour and move so that it sits behind your subject.

THE RULE OF THIRDS

Over the years, a number of compositional "rules" have been developed by artists and photographers to make good composition easier. A good one that is easy to use is the "rule of thirds". This is so popular that some cameras can even display superimposed lines over the scene that match the rule of thirds. You do not always have to use the idea of a rule of thirds, though, because the world does not always fit it. However, it is a good place to start for placing things in a photo.

Divide a Photo into Horizontal Thirds

In your mind, draw imaginary horizontal lines across the image in your viewfinder, or on your LCD, that divide the photo into thirds. Use these lines to position your horizon or any other strong, horizontal line. This helps get your horizon out of the centre of the image, which is a poor place for most horizons.

Divide a Photo into Vertical Thirds

Again, draw imaginary lines across the image in your viewfinder or on your LCD, but now use vertical lines that divide the photo into thirds. Use these lines to position strong vertical elements, such as trees or tall buildings. These are effective compositional places for this type of subject matter.

Use the Intersections

If you consider both the horizontal and vertical lines at once, you will find that you have four points where the lines intersect. These are great locations for your subject. These positions create interesting visual relationships with the rest of the photo, so you need to look at the rest of the photo beyond just placing your subject. The "rest" of the photo affects what the whole image looks like.

Rule or Guideline

The real world, or your view of the world, does not always fit the rule of thirds, in which case you should not force the composition into thirds. However, it can be a guide for how you place your picture's elements within the photo. It will especially help you get some variety in your pictures so that your subject is not always in the centre.

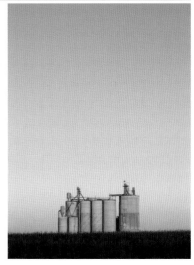

WHEN CENTRED IS GOOD

You may get advice from seasoned photographers to keep your subject out of the centre of the picture. This is certainly a reason for the rule of thirds and it is good advice . . . most of the time. However, if you always keep the subject out of the centre, you limit your options for composition. If you make a deliberate decision to either keep the subject in the centre or not, then you are more likely to find a good place for the subject in your composition.

Create a Bold Centre

Some subjects have a strong centre with radiating lines that all point to the centre. You can use that centre in a composition by putting it right in the centre of your picture and then getting in close. You need to get in close enough so that all extraneous details that do not relate to the centre and its supporting lines are kept out of the photograph.

Find a Balanced Composition

You will find some subjects that simply have a balance between top and bottom or side to side. Find a way to emphasise that balance by putting a centre found in the subject in the middle of the photo. For example, if the subject is balanced left and right, put the subject so that it is centred in the photo in the same way, left to right.

Balance Night and Day

There is a point in the sunset where the sun is right at the horizon. This is truly a balance point between night and day. You can put the horizon and the sun right in the middle of the picture if the top and bottom have detail to support the composition, such as a water scene. Otherwise, put the sun in the middle from left to right, but at the bottom of the photo so that the sky is emphasised.

Look for Patterns

Patterns that work from the centre can be fascinating for a composition. Sometimes the subject has naturally concentric patterns, such as a snail's shell, but other times those forms come from the way you line up objects in a scene. These can all make fascinating photographs.

WHERE HEADS BELONG

People take pictures of people – such as friends, family, and people in groups. People are shot as portraits to remember someone, as candid shots from events, as parts of a larger scene, and in many other types of image. Sometimes these are single-person shots, while others are shots of families or teams. People as subjects are one of the most common reasons for taking a picture. You can get better people pictures by paying attention to where you place their heads.

Keep Headroom Tight

You will often see people pictures with the heads centred in the photo and a big space over their heads – too much headroom. Unless there is a good reason for putting space over a head (such as a frame being there), keep the space tight and to a minimum, but without touching the head to the top of the image area.

Crop a Head to Show a Face

You may notice that a dramatic effect often used by television news is to crop the photo of someone being interviewed so that you cannot see the top of their head. This forces the viewer to look at the person's face, their expression, and their eyes, rather than just seeing an outline of the head.

Keep the Back Row of Heads Close to the Top

Parents rush out to find and photograph their kids after an event, and often want to include a whole group of people. But then they put a lot of headroom above the top of the back row, shoving the whole team into the bottom of the photo. A better approach is to tilt the camera down so that the back row of heads is close to the top of the picture.

Centre a Close Portrait Left and Right

When you get in close to a subject, you will often find that it looks best when balanced on left and right. You do want to keep headroom tight at the top, regardless of whether the subject is a person, a cat, or even a flower. By balancing the photo left and right, you make sure the viewer really looks at the subject rather than the composition.

WATCH YOUR EDGES

It is easy to get so caught up in your subject and making sure it looks right that you forget to look at the edges of the picture. However, those edges can be extremely important and will affect how viewers look at and perceive your photograph. Sometimes those edges can cause major problems when they include elements that do not belong in the image. You need to have edges that work with, not against, your photo.

Scan the Edges for Distractions

Distractions, such as branches, feet, hoses, and cords, often creep in uninvited along the edges of a photograph and call attention to their presence. Check edges regularly, including in playback on the LCD, and watch for distractions that need to be kept out of the photo.

Create a Photo with All the Detail on the Edges

One way to really learn to watch the edges is to actually do a little exercise with the edges of the photograph. Try giving yourself a project to take ten pictures that not only keep the subject out of the centre of the photo but also only have important detail along the edges of the picture.

Lead the Viewer in from the Edge

You will often find scenes that you can compose with something coming from the edge of the photo, such as a stream, that progresses into the image area in such a way that it draws in the viewer's eye as well. Curving lines can be particularly effective and pleasing when they do this.

Deliberately Crop a Subject at the Edge

The French impressionist painter Degas was famous for his paintings of ballerinas, where he deliberately cut off figures right at the edge of the frame. Photographers often get subjects touching the edge inadvertently. That creates a weak composition. Strength can come from really looking and thinking about an edge and how it affects the scene.

SHOOT VERTICALS AND HORIZONTALS

Cameras are made to shoot horizontally. Many cameras are even awkward to hold any other way. So it is no surprise that verticals are not as easy to do and so, of course, they are not done as often. Yet the world is both vertical and horizontal, so why should your photographs not reflect that? In addition, when you have both vertical and horizontal photographs of your subject, you know that you are looking for better ways of capturing that subject.

Experiment with Holding a Camera Vertically

In order to get vertical photographs, you have to be comfortable with holding your camera vertically. If it feels too awkward, you will not do it. Try turning the camera vertical and think about how it feels. Discover the best way for you to hold the camera vertically. Find the easiest way for you to reach the shutter, even if you have to use a different finger from normal.

Shoot Vertical Subjects Vertically

This may seem obvious, but cameras have such a strong horizontal orientation that many photographers just give into that orientation, no matter what the subject looks like. Just remember to think vertically with vertical subjects.

Shoot Vertical Subjects Horizontally

Once you start shooting vertically, though, it is easy to forget to do horizontal shots. This is important because your photos will start to look a bit boring if you shoot all horizontal subjects horizontally and all vertical subjects vertically. The point is to mix it up a bit, but to be sure that verticals get both horizontal and vertical coverage.

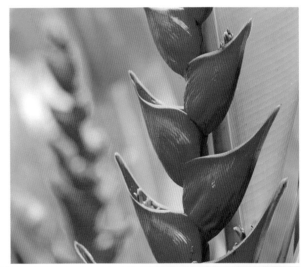

Shoot Horizontal Subjects Vertically

Something that very few photographers do is to shoot horizontal subjects vertically. It can be hard to do, but it can also create interesting photos that are very graphic and even abstract. When you start trying to place horizontal subjects in a vertical photo, you have truly arrived at looking for both vertical and horizontal compositions.

CONTENTS

3

USING LIGHT TO YOUR ADVANTAGE

Light – it is what makes photography work. Without light of some sort, you cannot take pictures. But light is not some absolute, unchanging thing. Light can be strong or weak, colourful or dull, contrasty or flat. Light changes as you change your angle to a subject or change the time of day that you shoot.

In this chapter, you learn literally to see the light on your subject and how it appears in a photograph. You learn what helps and hurts a picture so that you can control that light and take better photographs. Light can be a villain, but with a little study, you can turn it into a constant friend.

SEE THE LIGHT

Beginner photographers concentrate so much on the subject that they do not always see other things, such as the light on the subject and its surroundings. That light can be more important than the subject itself because the wrong light can make the subject almost disappear from view, while the right light can make the subject the star of your picture. Start "seeing the light" and you will find immediately that your photos get better.

Where Is the Light?

Start by forcing yourself to go beyond putting the subject into your picture. Make yourself look at the light. Where is the bright light? Where are the dark areas? Is the light where it needs to be in order to make your subject look its best?

Watch Both Subject and Background Light

You saw how important the background was in the last chapter. It continues to be important with light. A problem often arises when the light on the background wants to compete with the subject. Always remember that a viewer's eyes are attracted to bright areas in a background.

Notice Highlights and Shadows

Light is about bright areas and shadows. You must look at both types of light on the subject and background. Bright lights can help a subject or they can create harsh contrast where it is unwanted. Shadows can set off a subject or they can add unwanted contrast.

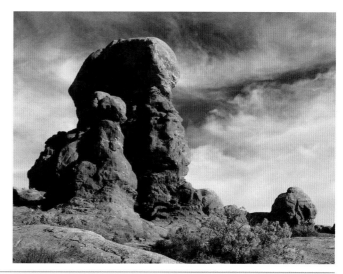

Use Your LCD Review

You have probably noticed how important the LCD is for getting better photos. The LCD can really help you see the light. Our eyes see light differently from the camera. Therefore, you can be fooled if you are only looking at the subject as you photograph it. Check the LCD review to see what the light really looks like in your picture.

SHADOWS ARE IMPORTANT

Shadows are critical to a good photograph and they only appear with light. Shadows can be gentle and open in their tonalities so that detail appears throughout them. They can also be hard-edged and dramatic while hiding detail within them. Either way can be both good or bad for your subject, depending on what the shadows actually do and where they fall. The worst thing is to have shadows make your subject less visible in a photograph. Seeing the light also means seeing the shadows.

Shadows Are an Important Part of Light

Photographers just learning about light can concentrate so much on seeing the light that they do not see the shadows. Yet shadows are as much a part of any light as the bright areas in a photo. Start looking at your subject in terms of both the light and shade, and how both can either make or break a picture.

Shadows Can Make Your Subject Stand Out

Very often, you can move around your subject so that shadows appear in the background and make the subject stand out. Shadows usually give a tonal or brightness contrast that helps the viewer of your picture to see the subject better. Even a small piece of shadow behind a bright spot of your subject may help.

Shadows Can Be Distracting

When shadows fall across your subject, watch out. The photo can become unusable. This is one place where an overemphasis on the subject can really hurt your photo. If you see the subject, and photograph what you "see," it is easy to miss how cross shadows or shadows in the wrong places can make a good-looking subject look bad.

Shadows Can Make Interesting Photographs

Shadows themselves can be a great subject. Shadows make interesting patterns all around us, and a photo of those patterns can make a wonderful image. Look for those shadows and how they play across the ground or on the side of a building. Then take your photograph up close and showing just those shadows.

LIGHT CAN HURT YOUR PHOTOS (WHAT TO AVOID)

This chapter has already given you several ideas about problem light and shadows. But if you do not pay attention to some distinct light challenges, you will not get the best photos that you and your camera are capable of. There are definitely some lighting conditions to avoid.

Beware of Harsh Midday Sun

That bright midday sun can be a real problem for photographers. It is a time of day when everyone is out, but the light is often filled with too much contrast between shadows and highlights. The shadows are also often in the wrong places for the subject to look its best. Sometimes you just cannot get a good photo at this time.

Watch Out for Hot Spots

The camera cannot handle the extremes of light that are common both indoors and out. Yet people can see beyond those extremes and see detail that a camera cannot. Do not get fooled by bright spots of light that end up as hot spots in your photograph. Look for them and, if you need to, check your playback in the LCD to look for them again.

Avoid Shadows That Cover Good Parts

A severe problem with light is a hard-edged shadow cutting across your subject in an inappropriate manner. That shadow can be very disruptive and distracting. In harsh light, these shadows can make it hard to actually see your subject clearly.

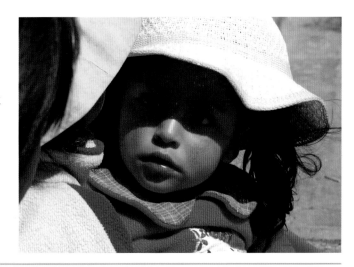

Avoid Light That Is Away From the Star

If you ever go to the theatre, you immediately see how the actors get the good light. The actors are the stars of the show – not the stagehands, not the orchestra, not the audience – and so the light favours them. This idea fits photography just as well. Watch your subject so that it gets the important light.

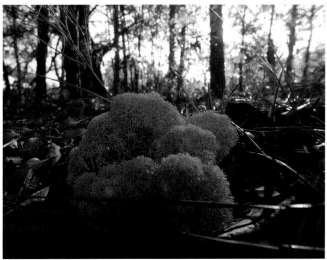

LOW FRONT LIGHT CAN BE BEAUTIFUL

Front light is light that is hitting the front of your subject, as seen from your camera position. It is definitely a light with many qualities, both good and bad. It is the light that people used to say you always had to have: light coming over your shoulder and hitting the subject. Today you hear a lot of photographers say that you should always avoid front light. You do not need to have this light or to avoid it but it can be useful to understand.

Front Light Can Be Boring

Front light is often boring because it has few shadows. The shadows fall away from the subject toward the background. Midday front light is generally not an attractive light because it is too high. It creates small, harsh shadows (such as under eyes or a hat brim) and flat light elsewhere.

Low Front Light Is Dramatic

When the light is low, it is less harsh than midday light and has a rich quality to its highlights and shadows. It can become like a low spotlight at a theatre and get quite dramatic when the foreground is in shadow and the background is dark.

Low Front Light Is Colourful

As the sun gets lower and approaches the horizon, it warms up and adds great colour to a scene. This can be a very beautiful light and you often see it used by Hollywood in films for a romantic look. It is an easy light to shoot in, although it can be hard on a subject's eyes.

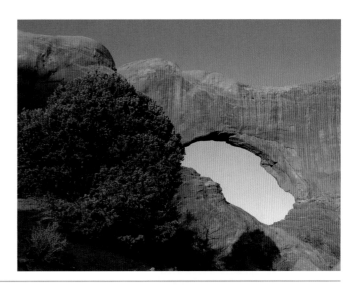

Low Front Light for People

A low front light can be very attractive for people. This type of light gets into the shadows on their faces, making eyes bright and filling in wrinkles. You may find that your subject has trouble looking into the light. Have them look down as you get ready, and then up and into the camera just before you take the picture.

MAKE TEXTURES SHOW UP WITH SIDELIGHT

Sidelight is light that comes from the side of both you and your subject. It can be high or low, which modifies its effects, but the important thing about sidelight – its ability to highlight textures and dimensions – never changes. Like all other light, sidelight is not arbitrarily good or bad – it all depends on what it is doing to the subject. It can be a harsh light that is very unforgiving to a subject or it can be the perfect light to show off details.

Make Textures Come Alive

Texture shows up when light hits the high points and shadow fills in between them. That is exactly what sidelight does. It can only brighten the high points as it is not positioned to fill in the low areas. This effect can be quite dramatic with a sidelight that literally skims the surface of your subject.

Use 3/4 Sidelight for Form Plus Texture

When a subject has dimension and form, a pure sidelight might not be best for it. In this situation, you might look for a light that comes from the side, but between you and the subject, for what is called a 3/4 sidelight. This type of light makes forms look good and still brings out textures.

Use 90° Sidelight for Strong Texture

When the sidelight is at a 90° angle to the axis between you and your subject, texture can get really dramatic. However, you do need that textured surface to be fairly flat and without a lot of dimensional shape. As soon as the surface gains form, the 90° light literally makes it look like it is cut in half from the light and dark, and so that texture is not seen well.

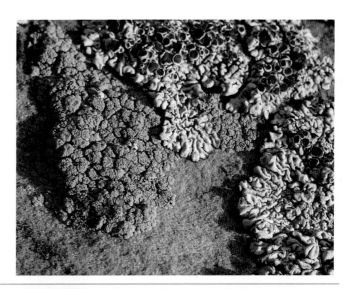

Sidelight Can Obscure

Sidelight is light filled with shadow potential – that is what makes the texture – but it is also light that creates shadows cutting across your subject. Be aware of that possibility and look for these types of shadows so that you can avoid them. Hard-edged shadows are the worst in this light.

SEPARATE WITH BACKLIGHT

A lot of photographers are afraid of backlight — light that comes from behind the subject and toward the camera. Years ago, amateurs always avoided it because the films, meters, and cameras of the day could not render it attractively. It is true that this type of light has its challenges but it is also a dramatic light that professionals use all the time. They use it because they can create images that most amateurs never get, because the latter do not want to shoot into the light.

Backlight Separates Parts of Your Photo

Backlight is a separation light. This means that it creates a lot of shadow. The light hits the tops of subjects or other parts of your scene and contrasts with dark areas just behind them. This helps these picture elements to stand out and become separate from the rest of the image, giving depth to the photo.

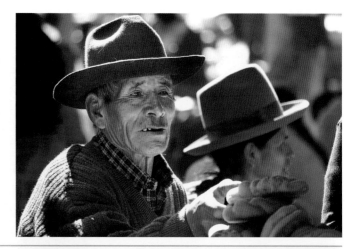

Backlight Is Dramatic

Backlight is always a light of bright areas and dark areas, highlight and shadow. Because of that, it tends to be a dramatic light. This is another reason that professionals like it. You can use that drama by looking for where the bright and dark areas fall on and around your subject.

Exposure Can Be Tricky

Whenever you have bright and dark areas close together, exposure can be a challenge. In general, it is best to be sure the bright areas have good detail and are not washed out. Check your LCD playback to be sure you have detail where it is important, and then change your exposure if you do not.

Watch Out for Flare

Backlight means that the light is heading right at you and the lens of your camera. That light can both create your photo and bounce around inside your lens, causing annoying flare. Use a lens shade when you can, to block extraneous light. You can also use your hand to shade your lens – just be careful it does not get in your photo!

ADD IMPACT WITH SPOTLIGHT

You know what it means to be "in the spotlight". It is a theatrical expression that says you are getting more attention. Often that is exactly what you want to do with your photographs – give your subject more attention. Many lights can act like a spotlight and give that added attention to your subject by putting it in the light, while the rest of the scene is in darkness. Shadows can be as important as light in order to set off your subject.

A Spotlight Is Like a Theatrical Light

The lights dim and a spot of light appears on an actor. You know immediately where to look and where your attention should be. Light can do the same for your photographs; create a spot of light that tells your viewer exactly where to look in your picture.

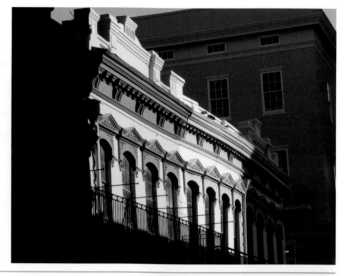

Spotlight Can Clearly Show Your Subject

In the theatrical example, you know that the spot-lit actor or action really stands out clearly on the stage. When you can find a spot of light on your subject, that same effect occurs and you ensure that the viewer of your image can clearly see the subject.

Spotlight Can Make a Scene More Interesting

Sometimes a scene that gains a spotlight just picks up interest from the drama that it provides. Many scenes look a little flat in average light. But when the sun changes its angle to the scene, spots of light appear that give life to the scene. Even very average-looking scenes can gain excitement from this light.

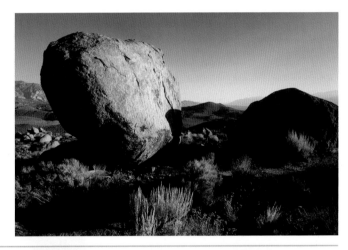

More Exposure Challenges

Spotlights on a scene mean contrast between the bright and dark areas. Anytime you have this contrast, you can have exposure problems. The most common problem to watch for is too much exposure that makes the spot-lit area look too bright or even washes it out.

TURN ON YOUR FLASH WHEN THE LIGHT IS HARSH

Nearly all digital cameras have a built-in flash. Many photographers do not know that they can use their flash at all times, including during the day. Keep in mind that your built-in flash is light that is always available and can help you out when the light gets harsh and unattractive. It is easy to turn on the flash and just try it, even if it does not always help. Believe it or not, every photo in this section uses flash in some way.

Brighten a Subject on a Dull Day

Sometimes the light just will not cooperate. The day is dull, the sky is lifeless, and the colours just do not look lively. Try your flash to boost those colours. It mainly affects things closer to the camera but that is often just what is needed to make the scene look good.

Flash Can Make a Dark Subject Bright

A problem in certain kinds of light is that the subject can get very dark. Photographing a subject against a bright background, such as a sky, can make the subject look very dark if the sky looks good. The flash can brighten the subject to a good level, while the camera still keeps the background from getting washed out.

Flash Can Change a Scene

Sometimes a background just does not look great. You can make it dark by using your camera's Manual exposure setting and underexposing the scene. If you are not sure how to do this, just try some settings and see what happens in the LCD. Then turn on the flash and use it normally to give a good light on your subject.

 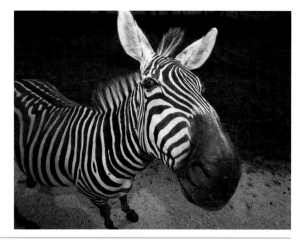

Try a Flash Off the Camera

Many digital SLRs have the capability to wirelessly work with a separate flash off the camera. All digital SLRs can work with a flash that is attached with a flash cable designed for the system. This gives you a lot of possibilities to move the flash and change your light's direction, especially when shooting close up to a subject.

TIME OF DAY CHANGES THE LIGHT

Light is not the same throughout the day, yet many photographers insist on photographing the same way throughout the day. That can result in unsatisfying photographs. Early and late light is low in the sky and changes scenes. Midday light is high and can be harsh and unappealing if photographed the same way as early or late light. By becoming aware of how light changes during the day, you can work with light rather than fighting its effects.

Early Light Is Great Landscape Light

You often hear about nature photographers getting up early for the light. The low, gently coloured light of dawn is usually a crisp light that really brings out the features in a landscape. That low light can look great on landscape forms and textures. The good light is usually gone by mid-morning.

Use Midday Light for Close-Ups

Midday light can be harsh with ugly shadows because it comes from above. It can be very unattractive for large scenes, such as landscapes, and unappealing for people because of the shadows. However, it can work for close-ups because you can easily move around these subjects to find the best light on them.

Late Light Is Warm and Beautiful

As the sun heads down toward the horizon for sunset, it gives a warm light that is usually much gentler than sunrise light. This can be a beautiful light for many subjects and it is also a light that works well from all directions – front, side, and back – although how well it works depends on the subject.

Keep Shooting after the Sun Has Set

For many photographers, it is time to pack up and go home when the sun has set. However, the time after sunset can give excellent results with digital cameras. You may have to wait a few minutes but there is often a wonderful warm, soft light that comes from the afterglow of the sunset.

TRY OUT NIGHT LIGHT

Night photography had a lot of problems when film was the only option. Often you had no idea of what you would get from photographing a scene until you had the film processed. Digital makes night photography so much easier to do and so you can quickly master it. Night offers so many opportunities for some really different pictures that everyone else does not have. You will even find scenes that magically change from boring to exciting as the night lights come on.

Digital Cameras Make Night a Great Time to Shoot

Night photography had a lot of problems with film. For example, it was really difficult to get the right exposure or colour. Now you can just take a picture and look at it with your LCD to be sure you have taken an interesting photo. Digital cameras also really seem to dig interesting light out of even the darkest night scenes.

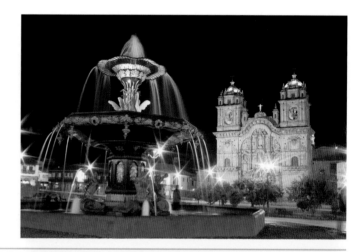

Change Your ISO As Needed

ISO settings on a digital camera can be adjusted for more or less sensitivity, which could never have been done with film. Use a high setting when you want to try shooting handheld and a low setting when you use a tripod. Even moderately high settings can look better than they looked on high-ISO film.

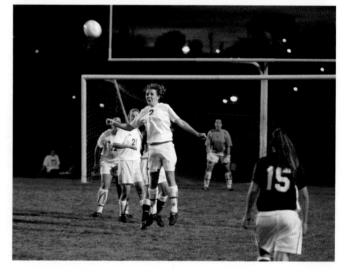

Support Your Camera for Long Exposures

Night often means long exposures. That can result in blurry photos unless you support the camera. A tripod is best but avoid flimsy tripods that are too light as they vibrate during exposure. You can also use an easily carried beanbag, which you can prop against a solid surface.

Look for Moving Lights

A really cool effect can come from night shots when you combine multiple-second exposures with a scene that has moving lights, such as a street scene. Those lights blur and create lines of light going through your photograph. You cannot fully predict what they will look like, so experiment with different times of exposure.

CONTENTS

4

UNDERSTANDING EXPOSURE AND WHITE BALANCE

Exposure is a basic part of photography. It is based on how long the light hits the sensor and how much light comes through the lens. A good exposure makes colours and tones look right in the photograph.

Today's cameras have built-in exposure systems that do a fantastic job. But tough situations can challenge that system. Your camera's computer cannot always tell what is important and what is not when the light on the subject is not average. In this chapter, you learn about exposure so that you can make adjustments that will help you consistently get better photos.

WHAT YOUR CAMERA METER DOES

A key to understanding how to get good exposure is to understand how your camera meter actually works. Most people think it is designed to give a good exposure. In fact, it cannot do that because a meter can only tell you how much light it thinks is in your scene. A camera meter does not know what kind of light is there – it cannot know the difference between bright light and a white subject, for example. Its measurements are based on the idea that the scene is average in brightness.

The Meter Only Measures Brightness

Most digital cameras have many tiny meters evaluating a scene. Each one can only measure the brightness of the light coming into the camera from that scene. A meter cannot tell the difference among such scenes as a dark subject in bright light, a bright subject in dim light, and an average scene in average light, and so it can misjudge the amount of light that is available for a photograph.

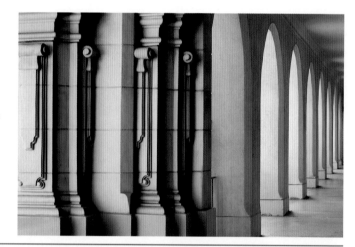

Exposure Is Based on Interpretations

The camera's meter does not give you an exposure. Your camera takes multiple exposure readings from the scene and uses its computing power to interpret the readings in order to give a good exposure. Cameras use information such as focus distance to give emphasis in that interpretation to the subject, which will be in focus.

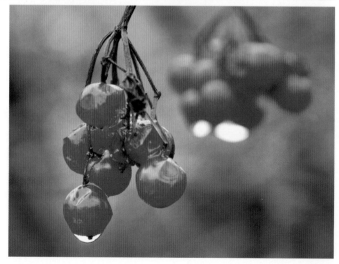

Dark Scenes Are Often Too Bright

When a scene is filled with dark colours and tones, the meter has no way of telling that this is not from too little light. As a result, metering systems give too much exposure to compensate for dim light. The result is that the scene is often overexposed, which can result in bright areas losing detail because they are too bright.

Bright Scenes Are Often Too Dark

Conversely, when a scene is filled with light colours and tones, the meter has no way of telling that this is not from too much light. As a result, metering systems compensate for this bright light by giving less exposure. The result is that the scene is often underexposed, which can result in highlights looking muddy and dark areas losing detail.

THE PROBLEM OF UNDEREXPOSURE

Underexposure causes problems for photographers. You may hear some photographers say that they can fix underexposure in Photoshop and so they do not worry about it. That is not a good way to approach photography. Underexposure creates some serious quality issues, including increased noise and weaker colour. Prints from underexposed image files look muddy and dark. Underexposure uses your camera's sensor poorly because it is not "seeing" the full range of tones that the sensor can capture.

Colour Is Lost

Bright colours get dark and dark colours get very dark. The camera cannot see dark colours the way people do and the *chroma*, or colour quality, of a colour can drop considerably. The result is that, as a dark image is brightened, it ends up with much weaker colour.

Watch Out for Bright Lights

Bright lights, such as the sun or a strong artificial light, usually cause the camera's metering system to underexpose a scene. The meter is just doing its job, telling the system it found something bright but then the system overcompensates and makes everything too dark.

Dark Tones Become Hard to Separate

When a scene is underexposed, the dark tones get darker. This means that they all cram together at the bottom of the tonal range, into the darkest tones. They can even disappear into black. Once those tones are crushed into the limited area of darkest tones and black, they can be difficult or impossible to separate again into different tones.

Noise Is Increased

Dark areas are where noise resides. Noise looks like someone sprinkled sand on your photo, adding what looks like film grain. So if an image is underexposed, much of its detail and colour ends up in that noise. When the photo is processed to brighten it and make the detail and colour more visible, the noise comes right along, and can become quite annoying.

THE PROBLEM OF OVEREXPOSURE

Overexposure is usually a problem in small areas. You really have to do something wrong to get a whole image overexposed and so this problem is easily corrected. What usually happens with overexposure is that the camera overreacts to something dark throughout the image area and makes it too light, which makes bright things way too light. Beware of overexposure whenever there are small bright areas in a large photo with lots of dark areas.

Highlights Are Lost

When too much light hits your camera's sensor, the brightest areas of a scene overpower its capabilities to capture detail. As a result, detail disappears. There is no fixing it in Photoshop, because there is nothing there to fix except for blank, white space. Blown-out highlights can be very unattractive.

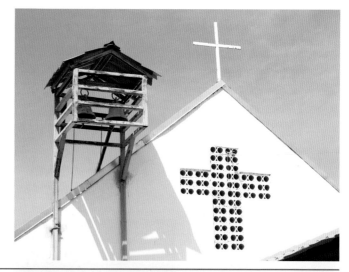

Colours Get Washed Out

As exposure increases, colours get brighter and brighter. With overexposure, they become so bright that their inherent colour starts to fade. Colours wash out, becoming pale renditions of the real-world colours. You can darken pale colours somewhat in the computer but that takes time and you still miss the original colours.

Shadows Are Too Bright

As exposure increases, shadows brighten, revealing detail within them. That is good if your photo is entirely in the shadows. But if your photo includes a larger scene with bright light, the shadows start to look unnatural and a lot less like shadows. Shadows need to be dark enough that they look like shadows in a photograph.

Overexposure Is Common with Dark Scenes

Dark scenes make your metering system give more exposure. This can be a real problem when the result is blown-out highlights, and shadows that are too bright. This type of image looks harsh and unappealing. Dark scenes need to be exposed in a way that keeps them dark.

CORRECT EXPOSURE PROBLEMS

Now you have an idea of how metering systems work and what exposure is all about. While your camera works to give you good exposures, sometimes it misses. You can see that the wrong exposure can cause some distinct problems for a photograph, from additional, annoying noise to washed-out, detail-less highlights. Your camera has tools to correct these problems. Some cameras have more than one but all cameras have features that help you get consistent, better exposures.

Use Your LCD

Your camera's LCD is a place to start when you check exposure. It is not calibrated the way a computer monitor can be calibrated but you can still use it. Look at small areas, especially if they are bright. Enlarge the photo so that you can see if the bright areas hold important details or are washed out and empty white.

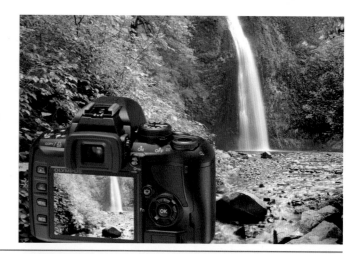

Exposure Compensation Can Help

Nearly all cameras have exposure compensation. This allows you to make the camera give more or less exposure than the metering system chooses. Add exposure by moving exposure compensation to the plus side and reduce exposure by moving it to the minus side.

Lock Exposure to Deal with Problems

Most cameras let you lock exposure to limit the metering system's changes. Usually, you just point the camera at something brighter to decrease the exposure, or at something darker to increase the exposure and then press the shutter halfway to lock exposure. You then point the camera back to your subject and the chosen composition.

Try AEB

Advanced digital cameras and digital SLRs often include auto exposure bracketing (AEB). This allows you to set the camera to take several photos in a row, each image with a different exposure, so that you can find the best exposure later. Set the amount of AEB and choose the continuous-shooting setting.

WHAT IS WHITE BALANCE?

White balance is a terrific new tool for digital photographers that gives your photos more accurate and pleasing colours by matching the way the camera captures them to the colour of the light. White balance affects how an image is recorded so that colour casts are kept out of your image. If an object is grey, it will look grey in your photo. If it has a colour, the colour will look accurate and natural.

White Balance Keeps Neutral Tones Neutral

White balance affects more than white. It makes all neutral colours, from white to grey to black, remain neutral. People's eye–brain connection makes neutrals neutral automatically, but a sensor does not do that. The camera has to be told how light is affecting neutral tones.

You No Longer Need Special Colour Filters

With film, you would need specially coloured filters matched to a film type to make neutral tones neutral. Without these filters, fluorescent lights made scenes look green and incandescent lights could give an orange cast to subjects. These filters could be used when the photo was shot or when a negative was printed.

Colour Casts Are Removed

Colour casts used to be a common problem with colour film. For example, the whole image would look like it had an orange or green haze to it. Digital cameras let you adjust them so that these colour casts disappear and a scene looks closer to the way you actually see it.

White Balance Comes from Using a White Card

You might wonder why this control is called white balance. Years ago, a video camera had to be told what neutral was so that it could balance colours to the light. Videographers would point the camera at a white card and set a control that would tell the camera to make the white a true white.

WHEN TO USE AUTO WHITE BALANCE

Your camera comes with the ability to automatically make adjustments to get rid of colour casts and to make neutrals, such as white, grey, and black, truly neutral. This is called auto white balance and is often shown as AWB on your camera. This is the default setting of your camera and works well in many situations, but sometimes it does not work as well as you would like. You need to know what it can and cannot do if you want the best from your colours.

AWB Makes White Balance Easy

Auto white balance is simple. You set nothing and so it makes the control very easy to use. The camera analyses a scene and tries to figure out what the light is doing to colours. Then it creates a setting for the camera that attempts to make colours look accurate and to show neutrals without colour casts.

AWB Can Cause Problems with Sunrise and Sunset

Your camera's white balance system has no way of knowing that a sunrise or sunset is supposed to have a warm colour cast to it. It just sees that all the neutral tones have colour in them and so it removes some of that colour and takes some of the life out of the scene.

AWB Works in Most Light

A good thing about AWB is that it works in most light. You can go from inside with fluorescent lights to outside sunlight and expect to get reasonable colours with your camera. AWB is really helpful when you are changing from one location to another or the light is hard to figure out.

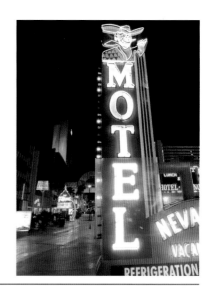

AWB Can Be Inconsistent

A problem with AWB is that it can give inconsistent results. For example, when you zoom from wide to telephoto, the camera may see different colours in the background and think that the light has changed. It then adjusts white balance when it should keep it constant.

WHEN TO USE DEFINITE WHITE BALANCE SETTINGS

Your camera comes with a group of preset, defined white balance settings. Even the most inexpensive cameras typically have these controls that take the camera off AWB, but most photographers do not know that they exist. Sometimes they are in a menu, sometimes they are accessed directly by a WB button. These settings define the response of the camera to a specific colour of light, although they can be used in other conditions for creative effect as well. They can really help you get better colour.

Defined Settings Lock the Camera's Response

When you set a specific white balance in your camera, you lock it down to that specific interpretation of the light. It does not change, even if you point the camera elsewhere, zoom the lens, or change your location. This restricts the camera's response to how it interprets a scene.

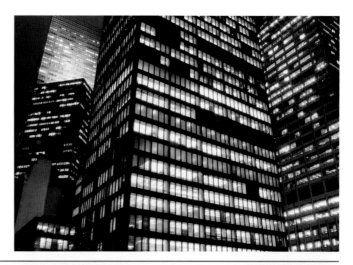

Defined Settings Are Consistent

With a specific white balance setting, you can zoom your lens in or out and be sure the colour of your subject's skin will not change. You can also move around a location and know that a change in the colour of the background will not throw your colours off.

Match Settings to Conditions

The basic way to choose a defined or preset white balance setting is to match the setting to the conditions. Choose Sunlight for sunny days, Cloudy for cloudy days, Shade for shade, and Tungsten for indoor light.

Warm Up Your Photos with White Balance Settings

You may like photos that are a little warmer in tone than the camera gives you. You can change your white balance to always warm up scenes. For example, try Cloudy for a daylight scene or Shade for a cloudy day and see if the colours look better to you.

USE WHITE BALANCE SETTINGS CREATIVELY

White balance settings do not always have to exactly match the conditions. You can use white balance settings for creative control that goes beyond simply making colours look more natural. You can choose presets that seem to be completely alien to conditions, just for their effects. There is no rule that you have to use the Daylight setting with daylight – no white balance police will arrest you if you use something different. And there is no quality effect from using something different.

Experiment with White Balance

You start with the Sunlight setting for sunny conditions, but there is no rule that says you cannot use completely different settings for your shot. Just to see what is possible, take a series of pictures of the same scene but with the white balance set to a different setting for each shot.

Use the Cloudy Setting for Sunset

Sunset photos are supposed to have rich, warm colours. This is an expectation that comes from how film used to capture sunsets. Digital cameras give much weaker interpretations of sunset unless you choose a specific white balance setting. The Cloudy setting always gives richer sunsets than AWB.

Try the Daylight Settings at Night

It would seem logical to use a Tungsten or Indoor setting for the lights at night. Yet that often gives such a neutral-looking image that the colours that you would usually expect disappear. You can get them back by using a Sunlight setting.

Create Blue Effects with Tungsten

Tungsten settings are designed for shooting with artificial light, not for daylight. This means that you can get unusual, often striking colours by using Tungsten for daylight. It turns daytime scenes blue. With a little underexposure, you can even make them look like night.

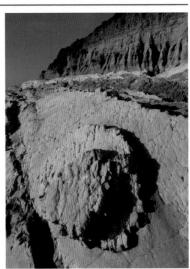

CONTENTS

5

CHOOSING SHUTTER SPEED AND F-STOP

Two basic controls change how much light hits the sensor in your camera: shutter speed and f-stop. Shutter speed affects how long light is allowed into the camera. Shutter speed is often displayed as just the bottom number – for example, 1/125 second appears as 125.

F-stop determines how much light is allowed through the lens. It is controlled by changing the aperture, the size of the opening in the lens. A larger opening, such as f/2.8, uses most of the maximum diameter of the inside of the lens. A smaller opening, such as f/11, uses an aperture that is less than the diameter of the inside of the lens.

CONTROL EXPOSURE WITH SHUTTER SPEED AND F-STOP

Shutter speed and f-stop work together to create an exposure for your subject. As a result, you have many options because the combinations of shutter speed and f-stop add up to a very large number of choices. You can potentially use each shutter speed with every f-stop, and vice versa, to match a huge range of brightness conditions. You do not have to choose every setting yourself because the camera helps you with specific choices, depending on the exposure mode you choose.

Shutter Speed and F-Stop Have a Direct Relationship

As shutter speed changes, a corresponding amount of f-stop must change in order to keep the exposure the same. The camera typically does this for you as you change shutter speed or f-stop with autoexposure. However, with this knowledge in mind, you can affect exposure by using different shutter speeds and f-stops.

F-Stops Change in a Regular Way

The most common f-stops are f/2, f/2.8, f/4, f/5.6, f/8, f/11, and f/22. The biggest is f/2, which lets in the greatest amount of light. The smallest is f/22,

which lets in the least amount of light. These are full f-stops and each gives an exposure that allows twice the light through the lens when you go from one f-stop to the next, such as from f/22 to f/16 to f/11, all the way to f/2. Each halves the amount of light when going the other way.

Shutter Speeds Change Intuitively

Shutter speeds represent the amount of time that light hits the sensor, such as 1/125, which may also be displayed as

125. A shutter speed of 1/125 is half the speed of 1/60, which means that it lets in half the light, and twice that of 1/250, which means it lets in twice the amount of light. Such a change represents a full step or full stop change. The stop refers to a full f-stop change in exposure.

You Can Choose Either Shutter Speed or F-Stop with Autoexposure

When you choose P (program) autoexposure, the camera chooses both shutter speed and f-stop. With A (Av or aperture-priority) autoexposure, you select an f-stop and the camera chooses an appropriate shutter speed. With S (Tv or shutter speed-priority) autoexposure, you select the shutter speed and the camera chooses the right aperture.

STOP ACTION WITH FAST SHUTTER SPEEDS

Fast shutter speeds stop action. If action is an important part of your photography, then shutter speed must be your main consideration. Aperture, or f-stop, is usually far less important. If action is supposed to look sharp – and it usually is – then you need a shutter speed fast enough to stop that action for the photograph. Exactly what shutter speed to use varies depending on the situation. You can choose that speed based on what you discover about the speed of the action. You can try different speeds until the action appears sharp in your LCD.

Movement Is About Time

Anything that moves is changing over time. A slow shutter speed shows how something moves during the time the shutter is open and you get a blur. A fast shutter speed captures a moment in time of that movement, a short enough moment to render the action sharp.

Speed of Movement Affects Shutter Speed Choice

Any action has a speed. A person walking has less speed, and therefore less movement through time, than a runner or a bike rider. Shutter speeds must be faster in order to stop faster action. You might stop someone walking at 1/125 second but a sprinter might require 1/500 second.

Angle of Movement Affects Shutter Speed Choice

Your angle to the subject also affects the shutter speed you need. If a moving subject heads toward you, you see less movement over time, and so you can use a slower shutter speed. As the moving subject changes direction and goes at 90° to your view, the subject changes very rapidly going across the scene, and so you must use a faster shutter speed.

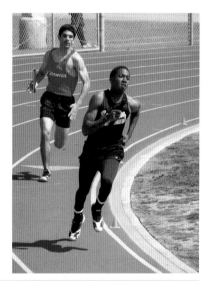

Timing of the Shutter Affects Movement

As shutter speeds get faster, such as 1/125 or 1/500 second, time is sliced into shorter and shorter moments. Movement is frozen because it is captured in such a short part of its time of action. There are many such moments in any movement and timing of your shutter release can change the photograph.

BLUR ACTION WITH SLOW SHUTTER SPEEDS

Shutter speed is not simply about stopping action. A speed can be too slow for a particular action, causing the movement to be blurred. This is obviously a problem if you want to stop the action of an athlete but get a blurry image. However, blurs can be used creatively and can show more of the world than we can even see. If you want to experiment with blurs, then be sure to choose a shutter speed that really blurs the subject. Slight blurs look like a poorly photographed subject or a mistake.

The World Is Not Timed to a Shutter Speed

The camera artificially stops action so that you can get a photograph. Movement can be photographed in other ways than simply stopped action, however. When you photograph movement over time, you get a blur, but you also see what movement looks like from a different timeframe.

Slow Shutter Speeds Create Blur

Slower shutter speeds mean that your shutter is open while movement and action occur. That creates blur. How slow a shutter speed causes blur depends on the movement. A hummingbird's wings can be blurred at 1/10,000 second but a snail is not blurred at 1/60 second.

Water Looks Great with Slow Speeds

Water is a classic subject for slow shutter speeds. This allows you to get those beautiful, smooth water shots that actually show the flow patterns of the water. Try shutter speeds of 1/2 to 1 second at first and then check the results in your LCD. You need a tripod or other camera support for slow speeds.

Blurs Can Be Creative

When slow shutter speeds are used on other subjects, the results can be unpredictable, but also quite attention getting. For example, try sports action at 1/8 or 1/15 second. Follow the subject as it moves and release the shutter as you continue to pan with the subject.

INCREASE DEPTH OF FIELD WITH SMALL F-STOPS

Many photographers seek to gain great sharpness throughout a scene. The choice of f-stop has a very big effect on sharpness in depth in a photograph, known as "depth of field". As you choose small openings or f-stops, depth of field increases. There is a trade-off, however: As the f-stop gets smaller, less light comes through the lens. This means that shutter speeds get slower, increasing the chance of blur. You often need camera support, such as a tripod, for maximum sharpness when you also want maximum depth of field.

Small F-Stops Have Big Numbers

F-stops are a little confusing because as they get smaller, the numbers get bigger. This is because the numbers actually represent a fraction, so while 8 is a larger number than 4, 1/8 is smaller than 1/4. This is exactly what happens with f-stops; f/8 is a smaller opening or aperture than f/4.

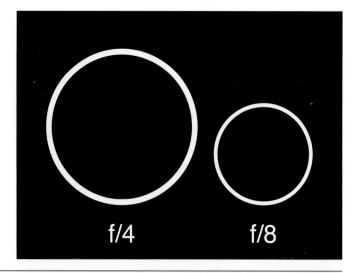

f/4   f/8

Depth of Field Is Sharpness in Depth

Depth of field represents the amount of sharpness in a photograph from near to far, or the sharpness in depth. A photograph that starts sharp with nearby objects and stays sharp into the distance has a lot of depth of field. An image with a very narrow band of focus is said to have shallow depth of field.

Small F-Stops Give More Depth of Field

As f-stops get smaller in size, depth of field increases. A smaller f-stop is represented by a larger number, such as f/16. Use those numbers to your advantage by remembering that larger numbers give more depth of field, regardless of the math behind them. Landscapes are good subjects for a lot of depth of field.

Watch Your Shutter Speed

You can set a small f-stop with aperture-priority autoexposure, or you can watch to see what the camera is doing with other autoexposure modes. You also need to watch your shutter speed. Slow shutter speeds are often needed with small apertures, which can result in blurred photos.

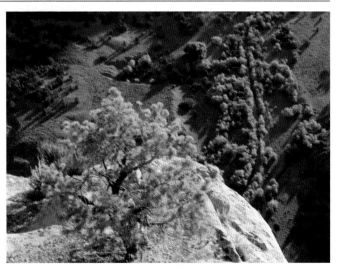

CREATE SHALLOW DEPTH OF FIELD WITH LARGE F-STOPS

While deep depth of field can be nice for a landscape or a travel scene in some distant city, it can be a problem with some photos. Your subject can blend into a background at times if both are equally sharp. For example, you may not necessarily want the background to be sharp and compete with your nice portrait of your son or daughter. Or, you may want to be sure your photograph of a flower actually makes the flower stand out for a viewer – it will not if the background is too sharp.

Shallow Depth of Field Limits Area of Sharpness

Shallow depth of field limits sharpness in depth. It does not change sharpness from side to side, but it does keep sharpness focused on a specific area of the photograph. This also helps the viewer focus on what is important in your image.

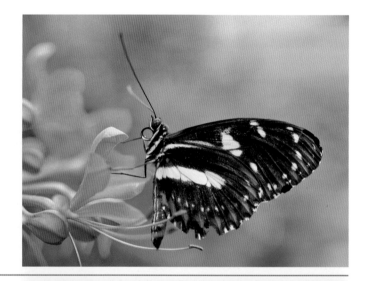

Wide Apertures Reduce Sharpness in Depth

A wide or large aperture in the lens reduces the amount of sharpness in depth that is possible in a photo. These are the f-stops with the lower numbers, so you can also remember this by thinking that a low f-stop number creates a low or restricted depth of field. The lower the number, the larger the aperture, and the less the sharpness in depth.

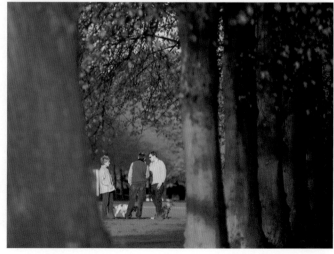

Telephoto Enhances the Effect

Telephoto lenses, or the telephoto-magnified portion of your zoom, give less depth of field at any given aperture. Conversely, wide-angles give more depth of field. Any time you want to decrease depth of field, use your telephoto lens settings and back up to get the subject into the image area.

Shallow Depth of Field Makes Your Subject Stand Out

So why use shallow depth of field? Because this always makes your subject stand out. The contrast from sharp to fuzzy is a helpful way of separating your subject from the background. Shallow depth of field is also what you see when focusing through a digital SLR.

ISO SETTINGS AFFECT EXPOSURE CHOICES

Light never remains constant. It changes in so many ways, but especially in brightness. Your camera gives you some control in how the camera responds to that brightness, in the form of ISO settings. These settings change the sensitivity of a camera to light so that the sensor records an image appropriately. Film has ISO numbers that relate to each film's sensitivity. In a similar way, ISO settings reflect how sensitive the camera is to light. The numbers change sensitivity in direct relation to their mathematical change; for example, going from 100 to 200 doubles the sensitivity of the camera.

ISO Settings Boost the Sensitivity of Your Camera

ISO settings on a digital camera are not exactly the same as the ISO numbers of film. Film ISOs were locked into a specific film. You can change digital ISO settings at any time. Increasing ISO settings amplifies the sensor's sensitivity to light so that you can shoot more easily in low light levels.

Low Numbers Give Highest Quality

Low ISO settings are based on the native sensitivity of the sensor and they give optimum colour and tonality. In addition, the lowest noise levels come from low ISO settings. The downside is that you often need slower shutter speeds, which can cause a lack of sharpness either from camera or subject movement.

High Numbers Allow Faster Shutter Speeds

Using high ISO settings is like turning up the dial on your radio to bring in a weaker station. Higher settings "turn up the dial" on the sensitivity of your sensor and allow you to shoot in lower light levels. The effect of specific high ISO settings varies from camera to camera, but they may result in weaker colour and increased noise.

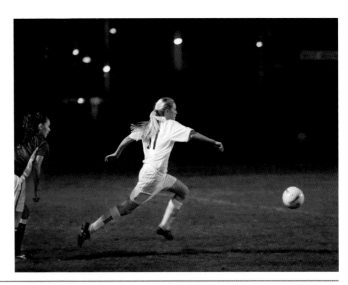

A Caution about Noise

Noise is a pattern of random bits of tiny detail that appear across your image. It looks like sand and is the digital equivalent of film grain. It can be a problem if it is distracting from your subject, but it can also be necessary if you are to get the shot. Noise always increases with high ISO settings and underexposure.

CONTENTS

6
GETTING MAXIMUM SHARPNESS

For most photographs, sharpness is a key element that helps make the image good or bad, useable or not. A lot of photographers try to "buy" sharpness by purchasing expensive lenses or expensive cameras, yet they are disappointed when their results do not match their expectations.

Sharpness might be considered a part of the photographer's craft. With practice, any craftsperson will get better in that field. If you try the ideas in this chapter, and then practise a bit with them, you will get sharper photos than someone who does not pay attention to these ideas, regardless of the price of their lens and camera.

MINIMISE CAMERA MOVEMENT

Camera movement during the exposure is probably the worst culprit for blurry photos. Small, lightweight digital cameras are easy to casually hold and shoot, yet a casual approach usually leads to less-than-satisfactory photos. For example, those little cameras can move very easily from a hard push of the shutter button. In fact, all cameras and lenses can have their photos degraded from camera movement or shake during exposure. Holding a camera properly to minimise camera movement is not hard to do; unlearning bad habits may be harder.

A Handheld Camera Moves

Obviously, a handheld camera moves. It has to because you and your hands move. However, many photographers do not consider that possibility when shooting. They take it for granted that somehow the camera will take a sharp photo and, if it does not, it is because the camera is cheap.

How to Hold a Digital Camera

You learned a little about holding a camera in Chapter 1. This is so important that it is worth revisiting here. So often, you see folks holding a little digital camera, with one hand waving in the air. This guarantees photos that are less sharp. Hold the camera with two hands and bring your elbows into the sides of your body for the most stable position.

How to Hold a Digital SLR

A digital SLR is held similarly to a regular digital camera, except for the placement of the left hand. Turn that hand palm up and place the camera down on the palm. Then grip the lens naturally. This is a much more stable position than if the left hand is palm down.

Press the Shutter

How you release the shutter does make a difference. You want to steadily press the shutter down until it goes off. As noted in Chapter 1, never jab the shutter or quickly lift your finger. Either movement can jar the camera and cause unneeded camera shake during exposure.

FOCUS ON THE MOST IMPORTANT PART OF THE SUBJECT

Autofocus, or AF as it is often called, is a great feature on all digital cameras. AF really does help to ensure that your photo is properly focused most of the time. This can be a challenge, however, when you are photographing up close. Then, the camera's AF system may focus on the wrong part of the subject because there are so many places to focus on, all at slightly different distances. Whenever you have objects at varied distances within your photograph, you have the possibility of the camera focusing on the wrong object.

Focus Is Narrow When You Are Close

When you get close – and this is not just for closeups – the area of sharp focus gets narrower. The actual point of focus becomes more obvious. This means that you must become more aware of where the camera is focusing and be sure that the important part of your subject is in focus.

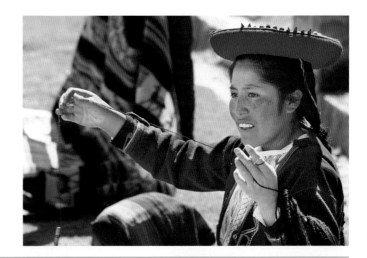

The Camera Does Not Know What Is Important

The camera and its autofocus have no idea of what is or is not important in a photo. It is simply finding something that it "knows" can be sharp. You have to tell the camera what is supposed to be sharp and so you need to watch the focus points and notice which ones light up to tell you what is sharp.

The Eyes of a Person Are Critical for Sharpness

In any portrait, formal or informal, the eyes of the person are a key part of that image. They tell a lot about the subject, which is why they must be sharp. If the camera focuses behind them and makes ears and hair sharp, then your photo is much less effective than it could be.

For Closeups, Check Where the Camera Focuses

With closeups, there are many spots on which a camera can focus and they are all very close together in distance. However, what can be sharp is limited because of the distance. You may have to press the shutter to lock focus, as described in Chapter 1, in order to keep focus on the important parts of the photo.

CHOOSE F-STOP OR SHUTTER SPEED FOR APPROPRIATE SHARPNESS

As you learned in Chapter 5, f-stop and shutter speed control exposure. How you choose an f-stop or shutter speed will change the sharpness of your photo, with f-stop affecting depth of field and shutter speed either stopping motion or allowing blurs. This is an important concept to understand when you are choosing either f-stop or shutter speed as your primary control. This section takes a look at both settings from a different perspective than in Chapter 5 — the perspective of sharpness, rather than the controls — so that you can better choose what you need.

Foreground and Background Need Depth of Field

A great technique for getting a better landscape photo is to find a foreground that relates to a bigger scene in the background. These images often look their best when both areas appear sharp. You can get deeper sharpness in such images by using the smallest f-stops and a wide-angle focal length.

Fast Action Needs Fast Shutter Speeds

When the action is fast, you must choose a fast shutter speed. Your camera typically has speeds of 1/1000 second and faster. Use them when you can if the action is fast. Let the camera choose a wide aperture if needed and use a higher ISO setting if you cannot get the speed you want.

Contrast of Sharpness Makes Sharp Areas Look Sharper

When you shoot with a telephoto lens and a wide f-stop, you limit your sharpness to a restricted depth in the photo. This allows you to contrast out-of-focus areas next to the sharp areas. These planes of contrasting sharpness can make your sharp area look even sharper.

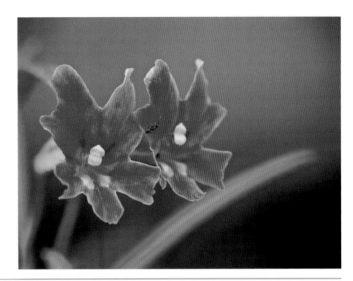

Pan Your Camera with Slow Shutter Speeds

With slow shutter speeds, you get blur with a lot of action. Try panning or following the movement with your camera and then shooting during that movement. This often keeps the subject sharp or, at least, less blurred, while the background blurs into an interesting, muted pattern.

GET MAXIMUM SHARPNESS WITH A TRIPOD

A good tripod is probably the best investment you can make for sharpness. You will not use it all the time, but it is invaluable when shooting at slower shutter speeds. Many photographers are surprised at how sharp their lenses really are when they see the results from shooting on a tripod. Even at moderate shutter speeds, such as 1/60 or 1/125 second, most people cannot match the results from a tripod without using faster shutter speeds. The blur might not be noticeable but the sharpness of details is affected.

Get a Sturdy Tripod

Too many photographers spend a lot of money on camera gear and then skimp when it comes to buying a tripod. A light, flimsy tripod can be worse than no tripod. Set up a tripod, lock it down, and lean on it. A sturdy, appropriately stiff tripod does not feel wobbly or as if it will collapse.

A Carbon-Fibre Tripod Is a Good Investment

There is no question that carbon-fibre tripods are expensive. But their light weight means that you are more likely to take one with you and use it as needed. With reasonable care, they last a long time and their cost is an investment in sharpness that will pay off over time.

Ballheads Are Easy to Adjust

The ballhead tripod uses a ball-and-socket mechanism under the camera mount to allow you to adjust the camera angle to the subject. A single knob locks and unlocks the head to move the camera. That single knob makes adjustment quick and easy but hold the camera firmly as you do or your camera may drop suddenly to one side or another.

Pan-and-Tilt Heads Offer Tight Control

A pan-and-tilt head is another common top for a tripod. It uses several knobs or levers to adjust the camera position. The multiple controls make it a little slower to use but some photographers prefer the control it gives over each movement of the camera.

GET SHARPNESS WITH OTHER CAMERA SUPPORTS

A tripod is not the only option for getting added sharpness when shooting at slower shutter speeds. Traveling with a tripod can be difficult if you must pack really light. In addition, a tripod can be hard to take to some places, such as when you are photographing a historic street with a lot of tourists who might trip over it. Some places even prohibit them. Tripods can also be awkward to carry and move around in some settings, such as at sports events. Luckily, there are alternatives.

Beanbags Make Very Portable Supports

Beanbags are very pliable bags that let you prop a camera against a solid surface. Some actually have beans inside, although most have plastic pellets. The bag molds against the camera to help you hold it stable against a post, chair, bookcase, parking meter, or any other convenient, non-moving object.

Monopods Are Great for Sports Action

A monopod is like one leg of a tripod with a head on top. These are great for shooting sports, as the monopod can carry the weight of the camera and lens as you watch the action develop. They can be used in a lot of situations where you need a slower shutter speed but cannot use a tripod.

Gorillapods Wrap around Objects

A relatively new product, the Gorillapod looks like a miniature tripod with bendable legs. It comes in different sizes for different sizes of cameras. While it can support a smaller camera directly, most of the time a Gorillapod is used by wrapping its legs around a solid object, such as a post. The unit itself is very lightweight.

Table-Top Tripods Can Help with Small Cameras

Miniature, folding tripods can fit into a camera bag and can be opened and used on a table or any other flat solid surface to keep your camera stable during exposure. The smallest ones can be kept with a pocket digital camera to let you shoot with slow shutter speeds anywhere.

CONTENTS

7

GETTING THE MOST FROM A LENS

The lens is a basic part of a camera. Without one, you cannot even take a picture. The lens controls what the sensor sees – how much of the scene, what is sharp or not sharp, and perspective. Compact and point-and-shoot digital cameras have built-in zoom lenses that change focal length. Digital SLRs allow you to change lenses for specific purposes.

The focal length you use with your zoom and the lens you choose for your digital SLR is a very personal preference. This chapter gives you some ideas on how to best work with a lens to meet your photo needs.

GET A BIG VIEW WITH A WIDE-ANGLE LENS

The wide-angle lens is often used specifically to get a wider angle of view on a subject. This is the most common use of such a lens. A wide-angle lens uses any focal length that lets you see a wider view than normal. It is helpful when you cannot back up and a big view is in front of you. Yet a wide-angle lens or zoom setting can do much more for you than simply get more of a scene. It can also be a useful and creative tool that changes how you photograph a subject.

Shoot the Big Scene

The world is a vast place but it can also often limit you as to where you can photograph. A wide-angle lens can help you get more photographs of those big scenes. Remember that the wide angle gets "wider" top and bottom as well as side-to-side, so watch what goes into the top and bottom of your photo.

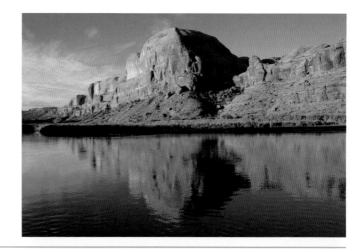

Go Wide Indoors

Digital cameras make indoor photography easy with white balance and ISO controls. A wide focal length lets you see more of the subject and its surroundings when inside. Rooms do not always give the photographer space to shoot easily and the wide-angle lens can really help to get everything or everyone into the shot.

Make Your Foreground Bolder

One thing a wide-angle lens always does is capture more foreground. Watch out for the empty, boring foreground that a wide-angle lens can easily capture. Get in close to something special and create a photo with a very strong foreground–background relationship, as described in Chapter 2.

Wider Angles Allow Slower Shutter Speeds

Because a wide-angle lens covers a large area of a scene, it stands to reason that any slight movement of the camera during exposure is less noticeable. You can often handhold a camera at much slower shutter speeds than expected if you shoot with the widest angle of your zoom.

GET A TIGHT VIEW WITH A TELEPHOTO LENS

Telephoto lenses magnify a scene. Whether you get such a view from a zoom or a single-focal-length lens, a telephoto lets you pick out and isolate details in a scene. You can really focus on things that sometimes cannot even be seen well with the unaided eye. Stronger focal lengths let you bring in subjects, such as wildlife, that are sitting some distance away, so that they fill up your image area. A telephoto lens is an important tool for capturing segments of a wide world.

Telephoto Lenses Isolate Subjects

A telephoto lens allows you to eliminate unneeded details as you zoom in. But it also changes other details, such as perspective and depth of field. This tends to make a subject stand out better against a background, isolating the subject out of the overall scene and helping capture that subject more clearly.

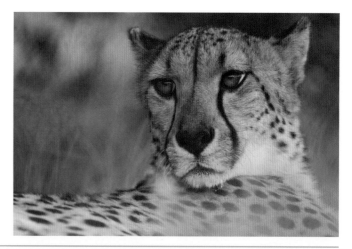

Watch Your Shutter Speed

Telephotos see a narrow bit of the world. Any camera movement during exposure will definitely show up on that restricted angle. You need faster shutter speeds for telephoto lenses so that you can stop that movement. Most people cannot handhold any telephoto sharply at less than 1/125 to 1/250 second.

Use Telephoto Lenses for Details

As you zoom in, you start isolating and focusing on the fine points of a scene or subject. The telephoto lens lets you find interesting details about a subject. Search out colour or texture that cannot be seen from a distant or wide view. Use your camera to extract information about your subject that other people miss.

Strong Telephoto Lenses Compress Distances

Ever see those photos of cars queued on a motorway? They are almost always shot with a telephoto focal length. Telephotos bring in the background and make it look closer to your subject. You get the strongest effect by zooming in and then backing up until the subject looks right.

ZOOM FOR BEST COMPOSITIONS

The zoom lens on any digital camera can be a great compositional tool. Composition is always about what you include in your image and what you try to keep out. Your zoom allows you to do exactly that: zoom out to include more details and more of a scene in the photo and zoom in to eliminate details that you do not want. You can quickly focus a composition down to its essentials by using your zoom to change what appears in the photo.

Zoom Out to Include Environment

Sometimes the important thing about your subject is not simply the subject but how it relates to its environment. Zooming out to a wider setting allows you to include more of the environment. In addition, depth of field is increased, which helps that environment to be more readily seen.

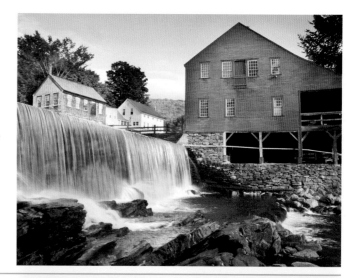

Tighten Your Compositions

One problem many photographers have is that they do not get close enough to their subjects; the photograph has too much space around the really important part of the image. Try setting up your photo how you like it and then just tap that zoom to magnify it a bit more. That will often make a stronger photo.

Zoom In to Focus on Your Subject

When the focus should really just be on your subject, zoom way in until that is exactly what you see and nothing else. You can make a subject look very dramatic if you get in close and use your zoom to its maximum magnification. If the subject is too pressed in by the edges of the composition, back up – do not simply zoom out wider.

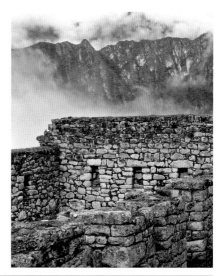

Experiment with Your Zoom Range

If you want to learn more about the capabilities of your zoom, here is a good exercise. Take a series of 30 photos, where each image uses a different extreme of focal length. Take the first photo at full wide angle, the next at full telephoto, the following shot at full wide again, and so forth. This can be a challenging and fun exercise.

CHOOSE FOCAL LENGTHS FOR DIFFERENT SUBJECTS

As you think about focal length, you will quickly discover that certain focal lengths seem to fit specific subjects quite well, such as landscapes with wide angles and wildlife with telephotos. It is worth keeping that in mind. While you can certainly photograph any subject with any focal length, you will find that some subjects are just easier to photograph with either telephoto or wide-angle lenses, but not both. It can be frustrating to try to force a subject into an image that the lens does not support.

Telephotos Are Great for People

Telephoto focal lengths can be very flattering for people. Try setting your zoom to its strongest point and then back up until your subject looks good. With most standard zooms, this provides a very pleasing perspective for a person's face. It can also blur the background so that the subject stands out better.

Capture Wide Landscapes

Landscapes are often big and you frequently have a limited location from which to photograph them. If you like photographing big spaces, a very wide-angle lens may be a necessity for you. You can get such lenses in certain compact digital cameras as well as digital SLRs.

Strong Telephotos Help with Wildlife

Wildlife does not generally sit still while you come up to photograph it. Even relatively tame animals are not comfortable with close approaches. You need a strong telephoto in order to photograph them. Common zoom ranges on compact cameras are typically too small to work for this subject.

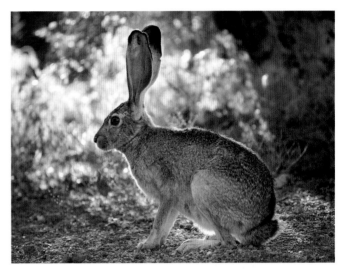

Wide Angles for Travel

When you are travelling, you often need to show off a scene, and yet you are limited in where you can photograph from. A wide-angle lens can be great to get a quick shot of a nice location without spending a frustrating amount of time finding a place to shoot from. Wide-angle lenses also let you show the whole environment of a scene.

CLOSEUPS AND LENSES

Closeup photography is a fun way to use your camera. All cameras today have the capability of focusing close, although some do better than others. Specialised lenses that are optimised for close work can be helpful but you do not need them to start to shoot closeups. Set your camera on its closest focusing distance (or set to closeup focusing) and move in to find interesting subjects for your photos. If you want to go closer, your needs may be as simple as a special closeup lens.

Try the Close Focusing Setting

Even the most basic point-and-shoot camera usually has a closeup setting that allows very close focusing within inches of your subject. This setting is represented on most cameras with a flower icon. Give it a try with some subjects in your area. Most zooms for digital SLRs also have close-focusing settings that you can use to create closeup work with those lenses.

Add a Closeup Lens

An easy way to get closer shots with many lenses is to use a closeup accessory lens that screws into the front of your lens. You can use these lenses with many compact digital cameras as well as digital SLRs. Look for achromatic closeup lenses for the best sharpness.

Extension Tubes Work with Digital SLRs

An extension tube is literally that: a tube that extends the distance from camera to lens. It allows all of your lenses to focus closer, although wide angles might not work. Extension tubes are very affordable accessories that open up closeup and macro photography for any digital SLR.

Macro Lenses Have Unique Features

You do not need a macro lens for closeup or macro work. However, such lenses do have advantages. They allow you to focus from a distance to up close without any other accessories or camera settings. They are also designed for maximum sharpness and detail when you are shooting very, very close to a subject.

FOCAL LENGTH AND PEOPLE PHOTOGRAPHS

Earlier in this chapter, you learned that telephoto focal lengths work well with people. This is true and you are always safe photographing people with such focal lengths. However, good people photographers use all sorts of focal length to control the portrait even more. You can get very unflattering photos if you use a focal length inappropriately, but all focal lengths work for people photos if you use the right approach. Do not simply use a lens to get wide or narrow; check the LCD and look at what it is really doing to your subject.

Wide Angles Show a Person's Setting

As you learned earlier in this chapter, wide-angle lenses let you add some environment around your subject. This can be a great way to tell a story about your subject by showing them in a personal space. Such images can bring texture and colour to a portrait by keeping the subject in context with their surroundings.

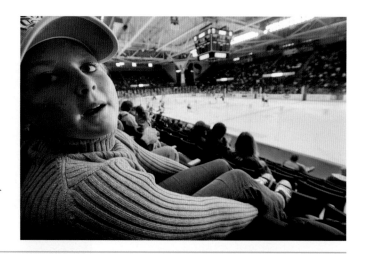

Telephotos Let You Isolate Faces

When you zoom in and concentrate on just a person's face, you make your viewer really look at that person. Such a close view focuses in on the eyes, a critical part of a portrait. It then isolates the face by keeping distractions out of the frame. The telephoto lens lets you do this while keeping a comfortable distance from your subject.

Wide Angles Up Close Give Striking Results

Many photographers shy away from shooting people with wide-angle lenses, especially up close. It is true that such a technique can give some wildly distorted looks to a face, which not all subjects appreciate. Yet you can also create striking images that grab you in a way that no other technique can do.

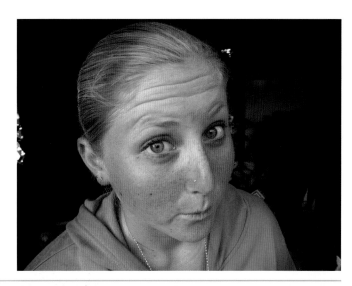

Be Careful of Focus with Telephotos

Remember that telephoto lenses have a limited area of focus. You need to be careful that your camera's autofocus is not focusing on the wrong parts of a face – for example, the tip of the nose or the ears. Work to be sure that focus is on the eyes. Sharp eyes really make a portrait more effective.

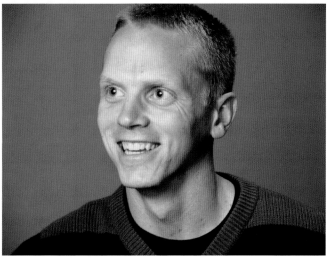

HOW TO BUY A NEW LENS

Lenses can be a seductive attraction for a digital SLR owner. There are many on the market and they all offer excellent results. That can make buying a new lens rather confusing. Each lens has its pros and cons related to specific photographers or subject matter, yet the glass can be so attractive that photographers end up buying gear that is not really suited to them. Here are some ideas for what to consider when you want to add a lens to your bag.

Look at Your Limitations in Picture Taking

The first thing to consider is what you feel is limiting you as a photographer. Do you wish you could get closer to wildlife? Then look at long telephoto lenses. Do you find you cannot get back far enough to capture landscapes you like? Then look into wide angles. Base your choices on what is challenging your photography.

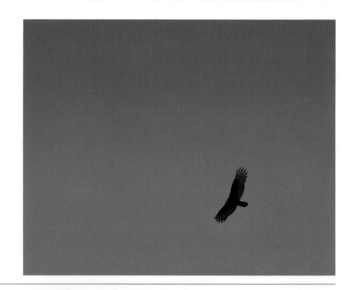

Be Wary of Other Photographers' Advice

It is quite easy to get impressed by another photographer's gear. They will tell you how great or bad a lens might be. Understand that lens choice and use is very personal and what works for one photographer might be wrong for another. Look at how a lens really might fit your needs, not just how it works for another photographer.

Expensive Is Not Always Better

Expensive lenses are better than lower-cost lenses, right? Not necessarily. A lot of factors go into deciding on a lens. A lens with a large maximum aperture such as f/2.8 for a telephoto will be very expensive, yet it might not be as good as the same focal-length lens with a maximum aperture of f/4. Large maximum apertures can be very expensive to produce.

Big-Range Lenses Are Great, But Not for Everyone

If you want to travel with one lens, you might want to get one of the big-range zooms, such as 18–200mm. That gives you a lot of telephoto and wide-angle focal lengths in one lens. However, such lenses are also generally quite slow, meaning that the maximum f-stop, especially at the telephoto end, is small and lets in less light.

CONTENTS

8

INDOOR AND NIGHT LIGHT PLUS FLASH

Conditions indoors change, from the time of day to the type of room to the kind of lights. With film, those varied conditions made indoor photography challenging. Night photography could be even worse. If you wanted to use flash, you could only guess what it would look like.

The digital camera has been a huge boon for dealing with the artificial light of indoors and night because you can see results as you take the pictures. You can now shoot good photos almost anywhere there is light.

DEAL WITH ARTIFICIAL LIGHT

Artificial light is the light you find indoors at home or at the office, in an arena, in a high-school gym, at night on the street, in a manufacturing plant, and in a restaurant. Basically, it is light other than sunlight. This light can be very interesting but it often presents challenges for the photographer, including sharpness, noise, contrast, light quality, and light colour. Successful artificial light photography requires that you learn to deal with those conditions.

Deal with the Sharpness Issue

When you go inside and at night, light levels usually drop, which often requires slower shutter speeds for exposure. If you are not careful, such a change in shutter speed can make images less than sharp, from the camera movement that occurs from handholding a camera, or it can mean that subjects are blurred from their movement.

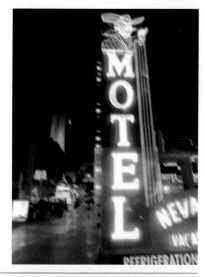

Light Colour Can Be Interesting

The colour of light can vary all over the place indoors and at night. This can be a problem when odd colours appear that are unattractive with your subject. On the other hand, the variation in light can be quite interesting and create images that cannot be captured in any other way.

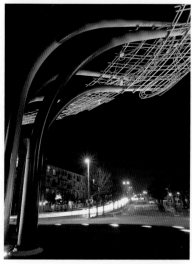

What to Do with Contrast

Your eyes can see more detail in a contrasty scene, such as night scenes, than the camera can but this goes beyond the night. You need to begin seeing in the same way as your camera and avoid angles and compositions that favour a subject as you see it but look bad as a photograph because of too contrasty a light. Use your LCD to see what is really happening to your subject in that light.

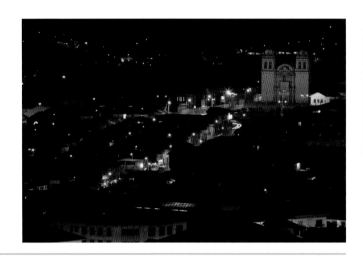

Why Noise Is Such a Problem

Low light usually means higher ISO settings, longer exposures, and, often, a risk of underexposure. All of these can increase noise to unacceptable amounts. However, sometimes the only way to get the shot is to use a high ISO setting and so you need to be especially careful of underexposure.

CORRECT COLOUR WITH WHITE BALANCE

Colour differences in light are often magnified when you get out of the sun. Just try photographing a blond-haired person in a room with both fluorescent and incandescent lights; their hair shows multiple colours from those lights. Artificial lights have so many different colours and their light affects subjects in both good and bad ways. You can continue to control this with white balance, as explained in Chapter 4, but the choices are not always clear cut indoors or at night.

Make Your Subject Look Good

If you are photographing a subject where colour is critical, such as a person's skin tone, choose a specific white balance to match the light on that subject. A viewer of your photo will tolerate all sorts of odd colours if a key colour looks good. Skin tone is one of those colours that really looks bad if it is off.

Create a Mood

Colour affects mood. You will find that certain scenes look better with a colour cast that influences the mood rather than a purely accurate colour match. For example, lights at night often look better when they look a little warm, rather than white balancing the scene so that they are neutral.

Emphasise Colours in Light

When you have a scene with varied colours of light, each light appears differently when you change white balance settings. This is a good case for not using auto white balance (AWB). AWB often gives you less effective colours because it tries too hard to compromise. Take some test shots and compare different white balance settings.

Try Custom White Balance

Sometimes the colours indoors or at night just do not look right, no matter what white balance setting you try. This may be the perfect time to use your camera's custom white balance setting. Use a white or grey card in the same light as the light that hits your subject and white balance on it.

Unfortunately, camera manufacturers have not standardised this process and there are many ways this can be done by the camera. Check your manual; usually it is pretty simple to do. For example, the manual may suggest taking a picture of a white or grey card and then telling the camera to remove the colour in it.

USE APPROPRIATE SHUTTER SPEED TECHNIQUE

Low light indoors or at night really taxes your camera's ability to use reasonable shutter speeds for sharpness. Even high ISO settings and wide-open lens apertures still result in slow shutter speeds. This is why night photos often do not look as sharp. The camera has too much potential to move during a slow shutter speed. Flash eliminates that blur but it also removes the feeling and mood of the light of a scene. There are some things you can do, however, to get sharper photos.

Watch Your Handholding Technique

How you hold your camera makes an especially big difference when the light is low. Be sure you have stable hand positions, with your elbows in, both hands gripping the camera, and the left hand supporting the lens of a digital SLR from below. Then press the shutter with a steady release – no jabs.

Use Wide-Angle Focal Lengths

Because wide-angle focal lengths can be handheld at slower shutter speeds than telephotos, they can be a real help when the light levels drop. Set your zoom to its widest as you shoot with slow shutter speeds. Never use telephoto focal lengths handheld in these conditions unless you have a lens with a wide maximum aperture.

Try Continuous Shooting

Set your camera to continuous shooting when the shutter speed is slow. Then take a series of photos by just holding down the shutter. Very often, one of those shots will be sharp when the others are not. You are not moving much when such shots are made and you cannot push the shutter release too hard.

Breathe Correctly

Many people think they should hold their breath when photographing with slow shutter speeds. That is a fallacy. Holding your breath can make you shake. Instead, use an old rifle shooter's technique: take a big breath and then let it out slowly, releasing the shutter as you do.

BRACE THE CAMERA FOR SHARPNESS

Anything you can do to steady your camera will help you get sharper photos when shutter speeds are slow. As day changes to night and you begin to photograph under changing light, there will be some point, depending on the focal length of your lens, where shutter speeds are too slow to hold steady without support. A tripod can help and can be an important tool for shooting at night, but sometimes you just cannot use one. In these situations, you have other options.

Brace the Camera Against Something Solid

You can almost always find something solid to brace your camera against when you are inside. Think about the possibilities: door frames, chair backs, shelves, lamp stands, tables, and more. You can often shoot at quite slow shutter speeds when you have a camera pressed solidly against a bookshelf.

Try a Beanbag with a Screw

Beanbags are wonderful stabilisers for a camera. However, they slide easily from under the camera when the support area is not flat. Bogen markets a beanbag called "The Pod" that includes a tripod screw in the middle. This lets you attach the beanbag so that it stays right with the bottom of the camera, no matter where it is.

Look for Anything to Steady Your Camera

When you set a camera on a solid surface, it is often not aimed right. Look for anything that could be used to stabilise the camera at the shooting angle. For example, you can use rolled up paper, a shoe, or added fingers. Be imaginative, as long as the camera does not wobble.

Tripods Give Great Results

When you want the sharpest results in low light, you have to come back to the tripod. A tripod keeps the camera from moving during typically long exposures. If your camera has a two-second self-timer, use it when shooting long exposures on a tripod, as it helps the camera and tripod settle from any vibrations.

UNDERSTAND HOW FLASH WORKS

As interesting as indoor and evening light can be, after a while, you have to use a flash. A flash is a controlled light in colour, direction, and intensity. It happens too fast for you to see anything other than a flash. The camera uses that flash to calculate an exposure that is correct for your subject and scene. In addition, you can always check your flash photos in the camera LCD to be sure exposure is right and to see if you have problems from the light of your flash.

The Camera Controls Flash Exposure

Cameras today have a lot of computing power built into them. A digital camera meters the results of a flash over multiple spots across the image area, compares those readings, and then calculates an exposure for the scene. The meter works as it does with normal exposures and can be overly influenced by light or dark subjects.

Digital Photography Needs a Pre-Flash

You may have noticed a double flash when you use flash with your camera. The camera sends out a first burst of light from the flash to see how much light is needed to create the exposure. It measures the light coming back from that flash, calculates the exposure from it, and takes the photo with that exposure.

Accessory Flash Offers Options

An accessory flash is a separate unit that usually attaches to a flash shoe on top of the camera. All digital SLRs can use them, as well as some compact digital cameras. These units have a lot more power and versatility than a built-in unit. You can also get many kinds of accessory for them that help control your light even more.

In-Camera Flash Is Helpful but Limited

In-camera flash is very helpful because it means that you always have a flash with you. You can turn it on whenever you need more control to your light. However, it is small and does not have a lot of power. It may have little effect on subjects that are farther than about 10 to 15 feet away from the camera and you cannot modify it much, such as by using a diffuser.

DEAL WITH RED-EYE PROBLEMS

Anyone who starts photographing people at night with a flash will run into red-eye problems. Subjects start looking as if they are possessed because their eyes glow red. This also happens with animals but their eyes have different colours, such as gold or green. Regardless, it is rarely a desired effect. It is distinctly unflattering for people, making it terrible for party photos, and yet that is where red eyes are so commonly found. Red-eye settings for a flash can help but there are other solutions, as well.

Red Eye Is a Flash Effect

Red eyes come from the flash and the flash alone. What happens is that, in dark conditions, the pupils of eyes get larger. This allows more light to get inside the eye. If the flash is close to the axis of the lens, it reflects off the back of the eye at the camera. The flash is so much brighter than the scene that this effect shows up in the form of red eyes.

Flash Away from the Lens Reduces It

Red eyes occur when the flash can reflect directly from the back of the eye to the camera lens. When the flash is away from that axis, its light cannot reflect directly back to the camera. The farther a flash is up from or to the side of the lens, the less likely you are to get red-eye problems.

Red-Eye Reduction Methods Sometimes Work

Digital cameras have a number of ways of trying to reduce the red-eye effect. Cameras sometimes turn on a bright light, including quick bursts of the flash, to try to force pupils to contract. This can be distracting to a subject. Some cameras include built-in red-eye processing of the image file that can work quite well.

Bright Light Limits Red-Eye

Bright light makes people's pupils contract so the flash cannot easily reflect off the back of the eye. While cameras sometimes offer this, it can be distracting. It is often better to ask your subject to move to a brighter spot or to have them look momentarily at a nearby bright light before you take their picture.

AVOID FLASH SHADOW PROBLEMS

Flash is a very direct light. Because it comes from a small but very bright source, it is called a specular light source. Specular light creates hard-edged, very noticeable shadows. Such shadows are neither good nor bad but, when they are not controlled, you will find problem shadows in your flash photographs. Shadows can be interesting or distracting, complementary or conflicting. You have to decide what you want to happen when you use flash for a scene.

Flash Creates Harsh Light

The first thing most people notice with flash is that the light can be harsh. This comes from both the contrast between bright and dark and the hard edge along the boundary between shadow and light. You can use this for creative effect but be aware that it can make subjects look too harsh.

Try the Night Flash Setting

Many digital cameras have a night flash setting. This balances the light from the flash with the existing light so that there is less contrast between the subject and the background. The background becomes lighter and the image looks less harsh. This means a slower shutter speed, so be sure to hold the camera steady.

Off-Camera Flash Is a Possibility

If your camera can take an accessory flash, it can also use a dedicated flash cord. This cord lets you take the flash off the camera for better-looking shadows and a more dimensional light on the subject. Some cameras even have wireless capabilities so that you trigger a flash off camera without a cord.

Soften Your Flash for Good Effect

A softer flash is a flash that has its light spread out. There are inexpensive, easy-to-use diffusers that you can attach to a flash to spread its light. These reduce the light a little but the camera automatically compensates for that. As the light spreads out, the shadows and their edges are less harsh.

BOUNCE YOUR FLASH FOR MORE NATURAL LIGHT

As you have seen, light coming directly from a flash can be harsh and unattractive. Yet this is not always necessary. Look at any fashion advertising; almost 100 percent of that is done with flash, but the flash is often bounced off a big, reflective surface. That bounce makes the light appear bigger, meaning that it spreads out considerably. It is this spread that makes subjects look better, with much more appealing light. The larger the light, the more sharp shadows tend to disappear.

Tilt Your Flash to the Ceiling

The quick and easy way to start using bounce flash is to get a flash that can tilt the actual flash tube part of the unit upward. Most accessory flashes allow you to do this. This immediately creates a large, gentle light source from above that is very natural looking. Be sure the ceiling is white and reflective or this will not work.

Turn Your Flash to a Wall

Many accessory flash units turn left and right. This allows you to bounce the flash off a wall. Look for a white or light wall. If the wall has any colour, it will show up in the photo. Warm white is okay. Bouncing light from the side gives you a very pleasant light with directional qualities to it.

Bounce Flash Makes the Light Gentler

Bounce flash works because the spread-out light on the wall or ceiling is large. This means that light can hit your subject from more angles, giving a gentle edge to shadows, yet still giving a very pleasing dimensional light. The bigger the bounce area, the gentler the light appears.

Off-Camera Bounce Changes Shadow Direction

With a flash-dedicated extension cord, you can get the flash off the camera and pointed wherever you need the light. You can then quickly go from a direct but very directional light to pointing the flash at the ceiling or a wall. That totally changes the light and gives better shadows.

CONTENTS

9

EDITING AND ORGANISING YOUR PHOTOS

Once you own a digital camera and memory card, it costs nothing to take a lot of photos. However, many photographers are now running into the problem of what to do with all those photos. With film, the prints and negatives were often stored in a shoebox, never to be seen again. With a little time and effort, you can access your digital photos again and again.

This chapter helps you get photos into your computer and then edit and organise them so that you can access them easily.

IMPORT PHOTOS TO YOUR COMPUTER

So you have taken a lot of photos, and now you want to get them from your camera to your computer. That will free up your memory card for new photos and give you access to your images on the computer so that you can optimise and enhance them, use them for e-mail, put them into a slide show, and much more. Once your photos are on the hard drive of your computer, you can do so many things with them. However, to start, you have to get them onto the computer.

The Computer Is Like a Filing Cabinet

Your photos may all be composed of electronic bits of information but what you are really doing when you move photos from camera to computer is similar to putting them into a filing cabinet. The computer is a storage place and you start using it that way by moving your photos into filing folders in the computer's hard drive, the "filing cabinet."

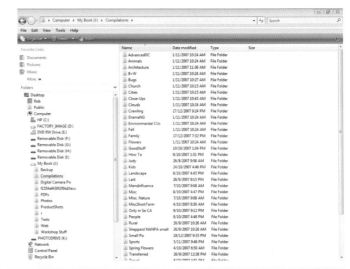

Download from a Camera

Getting your images from camera to computer is pretty easy. Most cameras come with a special USB cord that attaches to the camera and a USB port on the computer. Unless you have a very old computer, it will recognise your camera and its image files. You can then move the photos onto the computer's hard drive.

Download from a Memory Card Reader

Another way of downloading images is by using a memory card reader. This device plugs into a USB or FireWire port on your computer and then you take your memory card from your camera and put it into the card reader. The computer recognises the image files on your memory card and allows you to transfer them to the computer.

Advantages of a Memory Card Reader

A memory card reader offers a number of advantages over downloading from a camera. First, it is usually faster. Secondly, it needs no power and so it cannot run out of power while downloading, which can happen to a camera. Thirdly, it takes up little space. Fourthly, you never have to search for a "lost" camera cord.

ORGANISE PHOTOS ON A HARD DRIVE

Once you get a camera or memory card hooked up to the computer, you are ready to copy your image files to the computer. How you organise your hard drive is similar to how you organise a filing cabinet. Better organisation means you can find your photos more easily in the future. It also helps in transferring images to the computer because you have set up specific places for the photos.

Set Up Folders for Your Photos

Keeping in mind the filing cabinet analogy, you can set up folders in your computer that are specifically for your photos. How you set these folders up should relate to how you file and find anything in folders so that you are comfortable with the system. You want to create folders and subfolders that help you find your photos more easily.

Start with Pictures

A *Your operating system has a folder called Pictures, or something similar, already in your documents folder.*

1 Open the Pictures folder and create a new folder by right-clicking in the blank area and selecting New Folder.

2 Name that folder Digital Images.

This will be the home for your photos.

Create Folders for Events

Once you have a Digital Images folder, you can create specific folders inside it to help keep your photos organised.

① Create a new folder.

This example creates a folder for the year.

② Open the new folder and create subfolders for specific events or times you took pictures.

Click and Drag Photos

Once you have specific folders set up, it is easy to drag and drop photos from your memory card or camera into those folders.

① Open the new folder where you want to place your photos.

② Open the folder from your memory card and select the photos.

③ Drag them all into the new folder.

You need to create a filing system with which you can work and are comfortable. If you use someone else's way of working and it does not fit you, you will end up not using it for the best results. "A system you can work with" fits your personality and way of thinking. Create a folder for images on your desktop, in Documents, or on the hard drive. Any of these can work but only you know which is best for you. Set up a structure of folders within that folder that also matches how you like to think and work.

BACK UP PHOTOS ONTO A SECOND DRIVE

One of the big worries for a lot of digital photographers is losing photos. Sure, fire or water damage could destroy traditional photos, but the digital image is so ephemeral that it seems riskier. There is no question that hard drives fail, computers die, and photos become lost. The only way to protect yourself is to back up your photos in a location separate from your computer. Fortunately, this is not as hard as remembering to always back up as you photograph new subjects and scenes.

External Hard Drives Give Protection

External hard drives simply plug into a USB or FireWire port on your computer and instantly offer you a lot more storage. They are like adding extra filing cabinets. They are very affordable and come with a lot of empty gigabytes ready to hold copies of your photos from your computer.

Click and Drag for Simple Backup

1. Open your external hard drive.

2. Create a backup folder with a set of subfolders just like your Digital Images folder.

3. Click and drag your photos from the Digital Images folder on your computer's hard drive to the external drive by dragging a new folder into the right folder in the backup area.

Backup Software Can Help

Backup software automates your backup. There are many software programs that do this. Time Machine on Mac computers works very well to ensure you have a backup. The Save-N-Sync program from Peerless Software is a simple and inexpensive way to copy images from one drive to another.

① Choose the source folder.

   Ⓐ *You can click the **Browse button** (📁) to find your original folder of images.*

② Choose the target folder. This is the new place on your backup hard drive. Use the same folder names there as in the original folder to make the software run more efficiently.

③ Click Run Now to start.

Keep an External Hard Drive Away from the Computer

If you have some really important photos, you might want to keep them on a hard drive that is some distance from your computer. You can copy photos to an external hard drive for this purpose, and then move that drive to somewhere safe, away from your original system.

 You can rename a single photo by selecting it in Windows Explorer, pressing F2 *and typing in a new name. Typically, you want to rename a whole group of photos, though. Later in this chapter, you learn how to rename images using Photoshop Elements, an image editing program.*

USING PHOTOSHOP ELEMENTS TO ORGANISE PHOTOS

Photoshop Elements has a basic organising module that can help you keep track of your photos on your computer. Having specific, named folders always helps, but then you have to open and search individual folders to find a specific photo. By having them organised in some way, you can find exactly what you need much faster. Photoshop Elements includes several ways of doing this in the Organize module, such as using keywords, tags, and dates to help you find photos.

Start With Dates

1 Bring photos into Photoshop Elements from the Organize module by clicking File, Get Photos, and then From Files and Folders. In the resulting Get Photos dialog box, find the folder that needs to be imported by Photoshop Elements. The program creates references to those files, but no file is actually moved.

2 Photoshop Elements starts organising by using the date the image was shot, a date embedded in the file by the camera.

Rate Your Photos for Sorting

1 Under each photo thumbnail is a set of five stars. You can rate your photos to sort them into groups by clicking the stars. You can also click a photo and use the numbers 1 to 5.

2 Sort your images by star rating by clicking the stars at the top right of all photos and using the drop-down menu next to it to control what is seen.

Add Keyword Tags to Help You Search

A *The Organize panel contains a section called Keyword Tags. The preset tags are categories that Adobe has chosen.*

B *You can drag the preset tags onto your photos to tag them.*

① Create your own keyword tag by clicking the plus sign (**+**).

② Type a keyword name in the resulting dialog box. You can put it into an appropriate category.

③ If you click the check box at the left of each tag, you only see photos related to that keyword.

Group Photos into Albums

① Create albums for specific purposes such as family, church, or locations. Albums are also listed in the Organize panel. You can create albums by clicking **+** at the top of the panel. Then click and drag photos into the albums or albums onto photos.

② Clicking an album icon reveals the photos in it.

 Right-click specific parts of the screen to get a context-sensitive menu. If you are not sure about options for a photo, try right-clicking it; the menu is about photos. You get a series of options but they are limited and apply to the area you are interested in.

EDIT THE GOOD FROM THE BAD

Although it is useful to rate photos and separate good photos from ones that you want to delete, many photographers do not do this because the process is intimidating. What if they erase the wrong photos? Yet, if you do not get rid of photos, you clutter your hard drive with excess photos that take up space, which makes it harder to sort through the photos. It is very time-consuming and difficult to try to put huge numbers of photos into categories.

Get Rid of Exposure Problems

First, look for exposure problems. Overexposed, washed-out photos are never going to look right, no matter how much time you spend working on them. Underexposed, overly dark photos are also a problem, as they become filled with noise and are always frustrating to work on. Get rid of these images.

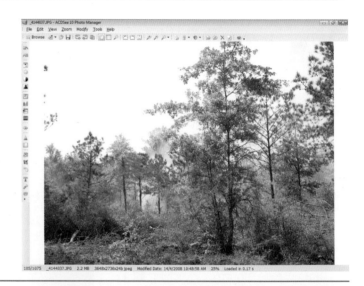

Watch for Focus Problems

No matter how much you like that photo from your last trip, if it is out of focus, you will never really fix it and it will never be a satisfying image. Blurry photos from the wrong shutter speed are difficult for most people to view. Delete photos like these, as they are just going to be problems for you.

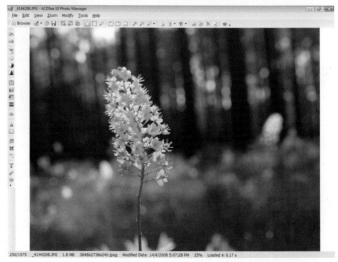

Remove the Shots with Bad Timing

Everyone takes photos that show bad facial expressions, with objects you never saw blocking the view on one side of the composition, or with the subjects in awkward positions. If you keep these photos, you will always be making excuses for them. Delete them, as they will never be effective photos.

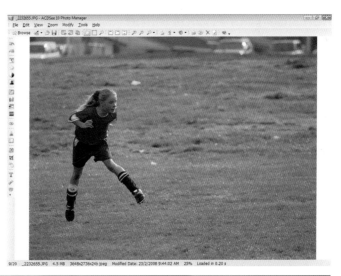

If You Do Not Like a Photo, Delete It

Many photographers hang onto certain photos because they think they might need them some day. They are usually shots of a favourite person, pet, or location, but the subject is not flattered by the shot or, for whatever reason, you just do not like it. Trust your intuition and get rid of the photos, as you are unlikely to ever really use them.

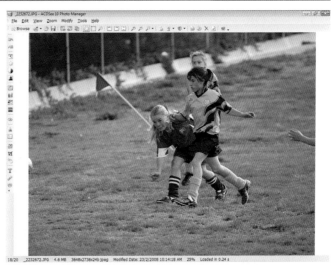

USING PHOTOSHOP ELEMENTS TO RENAME YOUR PHOTOS

The filenames for your photos coming from the camera are neither imaginative nor useful. The filename IMG03877 is not going to help you locate that photo later. By renaming your photos, you can search for those names to help you find them later. You can create whatever names help you describe your photo, but short names are easiest to deal with, both when searching and when looking at names in an image folder. You can always search for specific filenames by using your computer's operating system.

Rename Your Photos in the Organizer

① Select the photos you want to name or select all of them by pressing **Ctrl** + **A**.

② Select File.

③ Select Rename.

Note: *You can also press* **Ctrl** + **Shift** **N**.

The Rename dialog box opens.

④ Enter a name which will be common to all the file names.

⑤ Click **OK**.

 One way to help you find photos is to give a group of images a common base name that will trigger your memory. Photoshop Elements already has a function to find photos by date, so adding the date will not help you. Try things such as postcodes, people's names, and abbreviations for events that are memorable.

150

Rename Your Photos in the Editor

1 Select File.

2 Select Process Multiple Files.

The Process Multiple Files dialog box opens.

3 Click Browse next to the Source box.

The Browse for Folder dialog box opens.

4 Click the source folder containing your images and click OK.

5 Select the destination folder in a similar way.

Note: You can also click Same as Source.

6 Click here to specify options for renaming files.

7 Click **OK**.

 Renaming photos can be very helpful in giving you another way of searching for specific images. However, if you put your files into specific folders **for each downloaded set of images and structure those folders in a way that makes sense to you, having specific file names is not a necessity.**

CREATE A SLIDE SHOW WITH PHOTOSHOP ELEMENTS

Slide shows were a popular way of showing images in the days of film. Then, you had to choose between slide and print film for the photography, which would limit your ability to make a slide show. Now you can use your digital files for making prints, creating slide shows, and much more. Slide shows are a great way to show off your photos.

① In the Organizer, hold Ctrl and click the images you want to put in your slide show.

② Click Create.

③ Click Slide Show.

The Slide Show Preferences dialog box opens.

④ Choose a duration, transition and other options.

⑤ Specify the quality of the preview photos. Choosing a lower quality results in a smaller file size.

⑥ Click OK.

The Slide Show Editor dialog box opens.

 Photoshop Elements displays thumbnails for the slides and icons for the transitions.

Add Text to a Slide

① Click the slide to which you want to add text.

② Click Add Text.

The Edit Text dialog box opens.

③ Type your text.

④ Click OK.

Photoshop Elements adds the text to the selected slide.

The text properties appear.

⑤ Click and drag inside the text to position it.

⑥ Choose formatting options for your text.

 Traditionally, photographers would often combine vertical and horizontal photos in a slide show. That worked because the vertical and horizontal photos were the same size. However, with computers, you show the image on either a monitor or a digital projector, which give a horizontal form. This can make vertical photos look less good. It does not mean you cannot use both, but it does mean you need to watch how the two formats interact with specific images.

CONTENTS

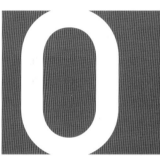

10

BASIC ADJUSTMENTS WITH PHOTOSHOP ELEMENTS

Photoshop Elements is a program designed to help you adjust your photos on your computer. Elements, as it is often called, is made to be photographer-friendly, yet it is also quite powerful in what it can do. Still, it does take some practice to be able to use it at its best. In this chapter, you learn some key ways of working with the Edit features of the program.

The developers of Elements have included many helps built into the program as well as an excellent Help menu. Look for text in many dialog boxes that helps you make decisions on what to do.

HOW PHOTOSHOP ELEMENTS IS ARRANGED

When you first open Elements, you get a set of choices, including Organize and Edit. When you choose Edit, you access the processing or editing features of the program. This is where the real work on a photo occurs, from adjusting its brightness to correcting its colour. It helps to understand how the interface is arranged, and how you can change it to make it work for you. Any changes you make to the interface are automatically saved so that Elements opens in that configuration the next time you launch the program.

Open One or More Photos

1. Click File and then click Open.

   The Open dialog box displays.

2. Select the images you want.

   If you open more than one photo, they appear in the filmstrip area at the bottom of the interface, though you have to minimise them to keep them there. Keep in mind that your computer may slow down if you open too many files.

Use the Toolbox and Toolbar

When a photo is open in the main work area, you can adjust it in many ways.

A. *The colourful toolbox at the left is important for many of the adjustments that you will make to your photographs.*

B. *You can change the tool settings in the toolbar at the top.*

C. *You can click the down arrow at the far left of the toolbar to reset the tool.*

Open Work Palettes

Ⓐ *The right panel of Elements is called the Palette Bin.*

① Click the Window menu to open and select additional palettes.

② Click Undo History.

Note: *The palettes that you have open are remembered by Elements the next time you launch the program.*

Change the Palette Bin

Ⓑ *Palettes open as floating palettes.*

① To add a palette to the Palette Bin, click the more button to display a drop-down menu.

② Click Place in Palette Bin when Closed. Close the palette.

③ Remove a palette from the bin by clicking the top bar and dragging it out of the Palette Bin.

④ Click the more button and uncheck the Place in Palette Bin when Closed option.

⑤ Close the palette.

You will find the best arrangement of palettes for you as you work with Elements. You may find that you need a certain layout of palettes when you first start and that you change this as you get more proficient with the program. Basically, you want to leave in the Palette Bin those palettes that you use all the time and close those that you do not. You can always open a closed palette at any time by clicking **Window** and choosing it from the menu.

YOU CANNOT HURT YOUR PHOTOS

Photographers sometimes get really worried about adjusting their photos in Elements, as they are afraid of hurting them. However, you can relax. It is very difficult to do permanent damage to a photo as you work on it in Elements. There are many safety features that let you back up and undo everything that you do. You really cannot hurt your photos as long as you do not save over your original files.

Know the Undo Command

The Undo command is ubiquitous in computer software — `Ctrl` + `Z`. Whenever your adjustments go astray, use those keystrokes to undo whatever you just did to your photo. Use the command again and you back up further in your chain of adjustments.

Note: *On a Mac, you use the Command key (⌘) instead of* `Ctrl`*.*

Protect Your Original

Use the Save As command when you open a photo in Elements.

① Click File and then click Save As.

This opens the Save As dialog box, which allows you to save a copy of your file.

② For a working file, save your image as a Photoshop (.psd) or TIFF (.tif) file, not as a JPEG (.jpg) file.

Use Your Undo History Palette

 If the Undo History palette is not open, click Window and then click Undo History to open it.

The Undo History palette shows you a list of what you have done to a photo and allows you to reverse adjustments you have made.

 Click any point in the palette to see what was happening to a photo as you made adjustments.

Save As You Go

Once you like what you have done to your photo, save it to be sure you embed those changes into the working copy of your photo. You can simply press Ctrl + S to save an image at any time. You can also use the Save As command to save versions of your changes if you think you might need to choose among different versions of your photos later.

A JPEG file is a compressed file format that can lose quality if it is opened, worked on, and resaved. Each time you open it, it has to be reconstructed from the compression; then, when you save it, it is recompressed. That can degrade the quality of your photo. JPEG can be used as a final, archiving format for an image if you need to conserve storage space.

You can open, work on, and resave TIFF and PSD files as much as you want; there is no quality change to the image file.

CROP YOUR PHOTOS FOR BETTER IMAGES

Often you have a good start to a photo but the whole image is not quite right. There may just be too much space around your subject so that you cannot see details as well as you would like. Or perhaps there is some distracting element, such as someone's foot or hand, that snuck into a corner of the photo and does not belong in the image. And there are always photos that look crooked and need to be straightened. Elements lets you take care of all of those problems.

Find the Crop Tool in the Toolbox

1 Click the Crop tool (⬚) to crop your image to show only the part you want.

Note: *The Crop tool looks like a traditional designer's physical crop tool.*

Drag a Box Around Your Subject

2 Click at the upper-left corner of the part of the photo you want to keep and then drag diagonally through the desired area. You do not need to be precise, as you can then click and drag the edges in and out as appropriate until you get the cropped area you need.

3 Click the green check mark (✅) to accept the change, or just press Enter. To cancel your crop, click ◼ or just press Esc.

Experiment with Cropping

The outside of the crop box dims so that you can see what you will keep after cropping. Try different amounts of cropping before committing to the crop. Even if you do commit and you do not like it, you can just press Ctrl + Z to undo it, which takes you back to the original photo. Then try a new crop and see how the photo changes.

Crop to a Specific Size

 Click the Aspect Ratio drop-down menu on the toolbar to display a list of some standard photo sizes.

 You can also type specific sizes in the Width and Height fields.

> **A** *Remember that you can reset all of these settings by clicking the arrow at the far left and choosing **Reset tool**.*

☑ **Generally, it is best to crop to a specific size at the end of your work in Elements, not at the beginning of the process. Crop out problems at the beginning so you do not have to deal with them as you work. If you crop to a specific size at the start, you may be limiting your sizing options later. You may discover that you want to have two different sizes. In that case, it is best to work with a master image that has had minimal cropping done to it.**

FIX CROOKED HORIZONS

Sooner or later, every photographer gets crooked photos. The most common of this type of problem is the tilting horizon. For example, the line of an ocean, lake, or distant horizon appears to take a downward slope that is not part of reality. Or you may find that your kids have a distinctive lean in the photo that is not normal to the way they stand. When everyone shot with film, you just had to live with this problem. Luckily, this is no longer the case and is very easy to fix in Elements.

Rotate the Crop Box

1. Create a crop box around the area of your photo that you want to keep.

2. Move your cursor outside of the crop box. The cursor turns into a curved arrow (↶). By clicking and dragging that curved arrow, you can rotate the entire crop box to adjust and straighten your photo.

3. Click ✓; Elements makes the crop and straightens the photo at the same time.

Line Up Horizons with a Straight Line

Horizons need to be straight and horizontal. Your crop box has two straight, horizontal lines.

4. Move the top or bottom line of your crop box close to your tilted horizon. Click outside the box to rotate the crop box to match the line and the horizon.

5. Drag the edges of the box until you get the crop you want, and click ✓.

162

Your horizon is straightened.

Use Custom Rotation for Precise Control

Sometimes it is tough to get the horizon or other lines exactly right. Elements offers a control for very precise adjustment.

① Click Image.

② Click Rotate.

③ Click Custom.

The Rotate Canvas dialog box opens.

④ Type in a number for the rotation. At first, you may have to guess, but if it is wrong, you can just undo it and do it again until it is right. You have to crop the edges when you are done.

Fix Photos in the Wrong Orientation

Most cameras today record orientation information with the photos so that they come out correctly horizontal or vertical. However, sometimes that does not work. You can correct that very simply.

① Click Image.

② Click Rotate.

③ Click 90° Left or 90° Right as appropriate for your photo.

FIX GREY PHOTOS

Often photos from a digital camera have a distinct grey cast to them. They do not have the lively contrast and colour that photographers have come to expect from film. This is not a digital shortcoming, but simply a way that camera designers have worked to hold detail in dark areas. You have to adjust the photo to bring back the contrast and colour. This can make an especially big difference in a print. With photos that you really care about and from which you want larger prints, always check these adjustments.

Try Auto Smart Fix

Auto Smart Fix is a one-step way to correct images.

1 Click Enhance.

2 Click Auto Smart Fix.

Although this may give you exactly what you want, it sometimes overcorrects colour. You can undo the step and try another control.

Try Auto Contrast

1 Click Enhance.

2 Click Auto Contrast.

You will often find your photo comes to life without colours being changed. This can be very important if you have a colour cast that is part of the scene, such as the light from a sunrise or sunset. You want the warmth of this type of scene to show in your photo.

164

Use Levels for More Control

① Click Enhance, click Adjust Lighting, and then select Levels.

The Levels dialog box opens.

Ⓐ *Look at the black and white sliders under the graph, which is called a histogram.*

② On most photos, you can move the black slider to just under the upward slope of the graph at the left, and the white slider to just under the upward slope at the right. This is a good adjustment to start with on most photos.

Black Is Subjective, White Is Limited

Ⓑ *The black slider in Levels is very subjective. You can get dramatic results as it moves to the right.*

Ⓒ *The white slider, though, quickly washes out highlights if you move it too far to the left.*

Printers, your monitor, and other ways of displaying photos all have the capability of showing a solid black tone. If your image does not have that solid black, your photo will not use the full range of colour and tone that is possible from that display. The result is that your image will look grey and less contrasty and will have less than satisfactory colour.

MAKE DARK PHOTOS BRIGHTER

As good as digital camera metering systems are, they do not make every exposure perfectly. Sometimes you get photos that are too dark and you need to brighten them. Or you may make a photo too dark from Levels adjustments. It may seem logical to use the Brightness/ Contrast feature, located in the Enhance menu, but this is a very heavy-handed control and not appropriate for most overall adjustments. Elements has controls that can make your photo look much better than that.

Try the Auto Controls

1 Sometimes for a dark photo, all you need to do is use the Auto Smart Fix command in the Enhance menu. This can really help with very dark and underexposed photos.

A *You can also try* **Auto Levels** *in the same menu. The two commands affect colours differently. You may find that you need one command for one photo and the other command for another photo.*

The adjustments you make are applied.

If you find the auto controls do not give you the results you want, then you can use an automated control that can be adjusted. The commands on the next page are found on the Enhance menu.

Use Adjust Smart Fix

1. Click Adjust Smart Fix.

   The dialog box opens.

2. Click the Auto button to get started.

3. Move the Fix Amount slider to the right amount of change needed for your photo.

Try Shadows/Highlights

1. Click Shadows/Highlights, and Adjust Lighting.

   The dialog box opens.

2. Adjust dark areas with the Lighten Shadows slider.

3. Correct bright areas with the Darken Highlights slider.

4. Fix midtones with the Midtone Contrast slider.

Experiment with Colour Curves

1. Click Adjust Color and then click Adjust Color Curves.

   The dialog box opens.

2. Adjust the sliders to brighten or darken specific tones, such as highlights or shadows.

3. You can also try one of the preset adjustments in the Select a style list.

CORRECT COLOUR EASILY

Colour is an important part of photography, so when a photograph has colour that is off in some way, people notice. In the days of film, this was a problem, especially when skin tones went bad or hair changed colour because of fluorescent lights. It is no longer a problem. You can correct colours quite easily in Elements and make any subject look its best under all sorts of light.

Try Auto Settings to Correct Colour

① When there is a slight colour bias to your photo, you can click Enhance and Auto Color Correction.

Elements examines the colours in your photo and tries to balance them.

Ⓐ *If you do not like the results, undo it and try **Auto Smart Fix** or **Auto Levels**.*

Remove a Colour Cast

① Click Enhance, Adjust Color, and then Remove Color Cast.

The Remove Color Cast dialog box opens. This is a very simple tool.

② Click something that should be neutral in colour (white, grey, or black).

Elements removes the colour cast. You may have to click in multiple places to get it right.

Adjust Skin Colour

① Click Enhance, Adjust Color, and then Adjust Color for Skin Tone.

The Adjust Color for Skin Tone dialog box opens.

② Move your cursor over the person's skin and click.

③ The Skin and Ambient Light sliders become active so that you can adjust the colour of the skin. You may have to click in more than one place to get the colour right.

Warm Up a Photo

In general, photos look better warmer than cooler.

① Click Enhance, Adjust Color, and then Color Variations.

The Color Variations dialog box opens.

② Select Midtones.

③ Move the Color Intensity slider to the left to lower the intensity.

④ Click the Increase Red and Decrease Blue boxes to warm up the photo.

TRY BLACK AND WHITE

Black-and-white photography used to be the most common way to take pictures. It has a very long history in photography but it nearly disappeared when colour photography became popular. Today, black-and-white photographs are enjoying renewed interest. Because it is no longer common and because it does not show the world as realistically as colour, it is used as a more artistic medium by many photographers. It is very easy to change colour to black and white in Elements.

Remove Colour by a Simple Conversion

1. Click Enhance.

2. Click Adjust Color.

3. Click Remove Color.

This is a simple way to convert colour to black and white. There are no sliders or options; you just select it and it works. Use this method for images that do not have a lot of important colours or that have good contrast from light to dark.

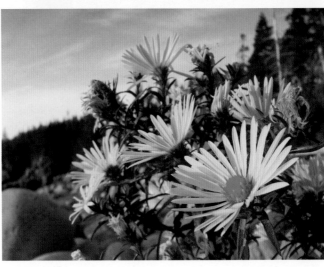

Control the Conversion

1. Click Enhance and then Convert to Black and White.

2. The dialog box gives you a whole set of controls to help you change colours into tones of grey.

   Try changing the Adjustment Intensity sliders to affect how red, green, and blue are changed into lighter or darker tones of grey.

3. Try the Select a style list for specific conversion results.

   Contrast is a critical part of black-and-white photography. Green and red are very different but they can look the same in black and white.

Adjust Contrast of a Black-and-White Image

Because contrast in a black-and-white photo is so important, you should make an additional adjustment after converting from colour. Often, all you need is the Auto Contrast or Auto Levels feature, found in the Enhance menu.

1. In the Adjust Color Curves dialog box, try changing the contrast by using the Increase Contrast style, making the dark tones darker and the light tones lighter.

SIZE A PICTURE FOR PRINTING

The size of your photo depends on the megapixels of your sensor. This size affects how large you can make a print. Cameras today are perfectly capable of making large prints that easily match anything that 35mm film can do. There is a certain range of print sizes that are possible with the pixels that come from your sensor. You can then make photos larger or smaller by having Elements change the number of pixels in the image file.

Choose a Printing Resolution

① Click Image, Resize, and then Image Size.

② Be sure that the Resample Image option is unchecked.

③ Type in 200 ppi for the resolution and note the size of your print shown in the Document Size area. Then use 360 ppi. These are printing resolutions that work for all photo printers and the resulting dimensions show you how large or small you can make your print.

Choose a Printing Size

① Specify a size for your print in the Document Size area of the dialog box.

Ⓐ *Ensure that the resolution is between 200 and 360 ppi.*

② Click OK.

You need to size all sides proportionately. If you need a specific size, then size one side to what you need, and crop accordingly.

Enlarge an Image File

Your photo might not be as large as you want, even when you use a resolution of 200 ppi.

① In the Image Size dialog box, check the Resample Image option.

   Ⓐ *Leave the resolution at 200 ppi.*

② Specify a key width or height that you need. The other dimension changes automatically.

③ In the Resample Image drop-down menu, choose Bicubic Smoother in order to add pixels for enlargement.

Shrink an Image

You may find that your photo is not as small as you need, even when the resolution is 360 ppi.

① In the Image Size dialog box, check the Resample Image option.

   Ⓐ *Leave the resolution at 360 ppi.*

② Type in the key dimension needed.

③ In the Resample Image drop-down menu, choose Bicubic Sharper.

Not all photos resize well, so save yourself some trouble and only resize photos that look good resized.

A photo that is over or underexposed frequently does

not look good at larger sizes. If your photo has a lot of noise, it often resizes poorly. Blur from camera movement also sabotages the resizing of most images, so do your best to get the image sharp when you take the picture.

173

SIZE PHOTOS FOR E-MAIL

Adding a photo or two to an e-mail is pretty easy to do. It is also a little too easy to add image files in their original size, which clogs up people's mailboxes and slows down their computers. Avoid annoying your friends and family. Resize your photos to a proper size for e-mail. This allows you to send the images with fewer problems and people will be happier to get photos from you. This is especially important if your recipient does not have a broadband connection to the Internet.

Make Your Photos Small

① Click Image, click Resize, and then click Resize Image.

The Image Size dialog box opens.

② Check the Resample Image option and select Bicubic Sharper in the Resample Image drop-down menu.

③ Type 100 in the Resolution field.

④ Specify the long side as a width or a height in the Document Size section. The short side changes automatically to reflect this amount.

This example uses a width of 8 inches, which is a large viewable image for e-mail. If you need smaller photos, you can use 6 inches.

E-mail a Printable File

① Type 150 in the Resolution field.

② Use a size of 6 inches for the width or height of the long side.

This gives an approximately 4x6-inch print at an acceptable resolution for printing, but in a file size that is appropriate for an e-mail.

Save Your Photos as JPEG Files

1 Click File, and then click Save As.

The Save As dialog box opens.

2 Select the JPEG format.

JPEG compresses your image file so that it becomes much smaller and is easier to e-mail. The JPEG format removes redundant data that can be reconstructed later when the file is reopened.

The JPEG Options dialog box opens.

3 Choose a compression level for JPEG using the Quality slider. Use middle or high numbers whenever you can.

A *To keep your e-mail small, try to keep your files to a maximum size of approximately 200 KB. If you are sending many photos, keep the maximum size lower.*

 Digital cameras produce large image files, even when you are using compressed files in the JPEG format. You can easily have a single file that is 1 to 2 MB in size. That is a very big file for e-mail. It may be easy for you to attach and send, but it is not so easy for the recipient to deal with.

 Keeping your files small for e-mail will make your recipients much happier to get photos from you.

...dy applied some sharpening to your image file. Still, most of the ...photo, you need to sharpen it after you have sized it for printing. ...bring the most detail out of your image file, based on the original ...t is not designed to make a fuzzy or blurry photo sharp. Sharpening ...akes them look worse.

Try Auto Sharpen

1. Magnify your photo with the Zoom tool (🔍) so that you can see what the adjustment does to your subject.

2. Click Enhance and then Auto Sharpen.

Use Unsharp Mask ?

You can use this feature when you need to control sharpening carefully.

1. Click Enhance and then click Unsharp Mask.

The Unsharp Mask dialog box opens. This control lets you adjust:

A. *Amount or intensity of the sharpening.*

B. *Radius or width of the sharpening.*

C. *Threshold or how noise is sharpened.*

Photographers' formulas for Unsharp Mask adjustments work for different purposes. Be careful not to sharpen too much.

② Try a range of 120 to 180 for Amount.

③ Try 0.8 to 1.5 for Radius, depending on how large your photo is.

④ Try 3 to 6 for Threshold, depending on the amount of noise in areas such as the sky and out-of-focus tones.

⑤ Click the main image with your cursor to set what is seen in the small preview.

Try Adjust Sharpness

① Click Enhance, and then click Adjust Sharpness.

The Adjust Sharpness dialog box opens.

② Specify Amount and Radius settings, just as for Unsharp Mask.

Note: *Because it does not have a Threshold setting, Adjust Sharpness is not good with images that have a lot of noise. However, it does a very good job for detailed subjects such as landscapes.*

③ Check the More Refined option to make edge sharpness look better.

STOP *Many amateur photographers oversharpen photos, making them look harsh and damaging fine tonalities that can give life to a subject. When the edges and tonalities in the photo start looking harsh, with strong, unattractive contrasts, then sharpening is too strong.*

CONTENTS

ADDITIONAL CONTROLS WITH PHOTOSHOP ELEMENTS

Photoshop Elements is a very powerful program. You do not have to know everything about Elements in order to get the most from it but you do need to know those tools and adjustments that work best with your subject matter, for your specific photographic needs. You cannot learn those things by simply reading a book. You have to practice and see what works best for you.

You can learn to use Elements by working with your own photos. That experience will help you use the program better and faster. Work with your good photos and your bad photos, so that you can get to know the program's tools.

USING SELECTIONS TO ISOLATE ADJUSTMENTS

When working on a photo, often only part of the photo needs to be adjusted, not the whole image. It would be great to be able to adjust only that part and nothing else. Fortunately, with selections, you can do exactly that. For example, you can make something darker or lighter, or adjust its colour, in isolation from the rest of the photo. Selections create a kind of fence around a part of your photo, allowing adjustments to occur inside that fence, but not outside. You can press **Ctrl** + **D** to remove a selection.

Shape Selections and How Selections Work

1. Near the top of the toolbox, you find selection tools, such as the Rectangle/Square and the Ellipse/ Circle marquees. Click and hold an icon to see both tools.

2. Select a tool. Click and drag the corresponding shape in the photo.

3. Once you have made a selection, with any tool, you can change anything inside it without affecting the rest of the image.

Try the Polygonal Lasso

1. Click and hold the lasso icon to see the Lasso selection tools: Freehand, Polygonal, and Magnetic.

2. Select the Polygonal Lasso tool (⬟) and click from point to point around a shape. Back up with the **Backspace** or **Del** keys.

3. Finish by clicking the start point.

Use the Magnetic Lasso Tool

① Use the Magnetic Lasso tool (⬚) to automatically find strongly contrasting edges of shapes.

② Click near an edge and move the cursor near that edge; the magnetic feature finds the edge for you.

③ Finish by clicking the start point or by double-clicking.

Make Quick Selections

① Use the Selection Brush tool (⬚) to brush a selection over a photograph.

② Change the brush size in the top toolbar to best fit your subject.

 The Magic Wand tool (⬚) creates a selection based on areas of similar colour and tone when you click one area. Select the tool from the toolbox and move your cursor over your photograph. Click on an area of tone or colour. The selection is based on that colour or tone. Change Tolerance in the options toolbar to get more or less of the area selected. Use Contiguous to select based on tones and colours that are contiguous, or together. Uncheck Contiguous to select similar tones and colours throughout the whole photo.

MODIFY YOUR SELECTIONS

You can modify both your selections and how you work on a selection in ways that make selections easier for you. You can build up a selection with a series of smaller selections and you can change the edge so that any changes will blend better. Selections can take a lot of time and make your work more tedious; these tips help you work with selections faster and more efficiently. Remove any selection by clicking Select and then choosing Deselect.

Add to a Selection

You often find that you cannot select a whole area at once.

① By pressing the **Shift** key as you use your selection tool, you can add to a selection.

② You can also click the Add to Selection icon (▣) in the toolbar so that you can add to a selection.

Subtract from a Selection

Conversely, you may find that a selection contains too much of an area.

① By pressing the **Alt** key as you use your selection tool, you can subtract from any selection.

Note: *On a Mac, press the Option key.*

② You can also click the Subtract from Selection icon (▣) in the toolbar to subtract from a selection.

Combine Selection Tools

Sometimes it is easiest to create a selection one step at a time, adding a little here and subtracting something there. These additions and subtractions are often best done with different selection tools.

① Try using the Magic Wand tool (🔳) on an area that contains similar colours and tones.

Ⓐ *This example uses the tool on a sky, with the* **Contiguous** *option unchecked to get the sky behind the trees.*

② Use the Polygonal Lasso tool (📐) with the Alt key to remove selection areas that are not part of the area you want.

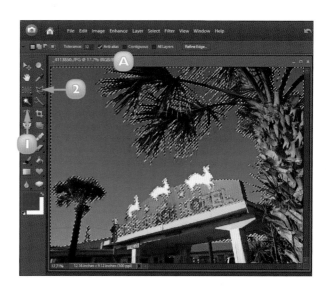

Blend Your Selection Edges

By default, selections have a hard edge that does not blend well into the adjacent areas of a photograph.

① Click Select and then choose Feather.

The Feather Selection dialog box opens.

② Use a small number for edges that need a sharper edge and a large number for edges that need to gradually change from one area to another. It is hard to give specific numbers as they vary depending on the content and size of your photo.

INCREASE COLOUR SATURATION WITHOUT PROBLEMS

When photographers first discover the Hue/Saturation feature, they often get carried away. This tool seems to magically transform dull colours into bright and vibrant colours. Unfortunately, that often means garish and unattractive photos. Also, overuse of this feature can result in more and very unattractive noise in an image. You can use this control effectively to give good colour without garish results.

Go Easy on Saturation

1 Click Enhance, click Adjust Color, and then click Adjust Hue/ Saturation.

The Hue/Saturation dialog box opens.

A The **Hue** slider changes the colours.

B The **Saturation** slider adjusts the intensity of colours. This slider is rather heavy handed; adjusting more than 10 to 15 points usually causes problems.

Change Colours Individually

The trick to using the Hue/ Saturation feature is to make stronger adjustments to individual colours.

2 Click the Edit drop-down menu to display a list of colours.

3 Choose a colour. Elements limits the adjustment of Hue, Saturation, or Luminance to just that range of colour.

Tell Elements Exactly Which Colour to Change

4 Refine your colour even more by moving your cursor onto the photograph. The cursor changes to an eyedropper (🖌).

5 Now place it over the colour you want to adjust and click once.

6 The colour scales at the bottom of the dialog box shift to match that colour so that changes are more specific to it.

Use a Selection to Further Limit Colour Change

7 Make a selection first to limit any change to a specific area.

8 Open the Hue/Saturation dialog box and limit its adjustments to a specific colour as described in Steps 2 and 3.

 Fujicolor film gave bright colours but they came from more than saturation. The film had a strong black base and deep contrast, which increased the intensity of the colour. You can get that by setting the blacks and whites (see "Fix Grey Photos" in Chapter 10). You can then use Hue/Saturation but avoid using Saturation alone for more than 15 points of adjustment. Tweak individual colours as needed to get your colours bright like Fuji film.

DARKEN SPECIFIC AREAS OF A PHOTO

Ansel Adams is a name that most people recognise as one of the great landscape photographers. He created wonderful black-and-white photographs of scenery that are still popular today. One of the things he did in the traditional darkroom was to darken parts of a photo so that it was more balanced and better emphasised and highlighted the subject. You can do the same thing with Elements and you need never find a darkroom!

Look at Your Whole Photo

Take a look at your whole photo and decide which areas are too bright.

① Find parts that look out of balance with the rest of the photo because their brightness attracts the viewer's eye away from your subject. These are the areas you want to darken, in such a way that the changes blend well with the whole photo.

Select an Area for Darkening

② Select the area or areas that need darkening.

③ Click Enhance and open the Feather Selection dialog box.

   Ⓐ *If there is a strong edge, the feather can be very small, maybe only a few pixels. If there is no strong edge, then use a large feather, for example 50 to 60 pixels, to blend the change more.*

Use Brightness/Contrast for Darkening

① Click Enhance, Adjust Lighting, and then Brightness/Contrast.

The Brightness/Contrast dialog box opens. In general, you should not use Brightness/Contrast for overall changes to your photo. For darkening, the Brightness slider gives a very good result.

② Move the slider left until you like the change.

Use the Burn Tool for Small Areas

① For small areas, choose the Burn tool (⬤) in the toolbox. It is near the bottom and shares the same space as the Sponge and Dodge tools.

Note: If you do not see the Burn icon, then click and hold on the **Sponge** tool (⬤) to see it.

② Set the tool to a range that is appropriate to the tones you want to affect.

③ Use a very low exposure of 5 to 10 percent.

④ Use a soft brush, sized correctly for the area.

⑤ Paint over the area to darken it using multiple strokes.

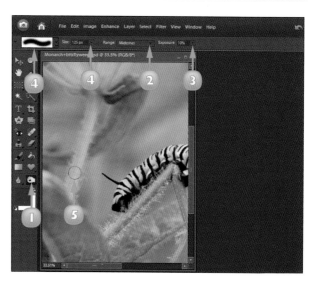

LIGHTEN SPECIFIC AREAS OF A PHOTO

Ansel Adams lightened parts of a photo to bring out detail in certain areas without making the whole photo lighter. After getting the overall image right, Adams would create wonderful, majestic photographs by selectively lightening and darkening the photo. He would sometimes spend days in the darkroom just perfecting the right proportion of light and dark areas. You can do the same thing with Elements in considerably less time.

Look for Detail that Is Too Dark

Take a look at your whole photo, looking for where darkness is working against your image.

① Which places are too dark? You can brighten these areas, in such a way that changes blend well with the whole photo.

Select an Area to Lighten

② Select the area or areas that need to be lightened.

③ Click Enhance and open the Feather Selection dialog box.

Ⓐ *Just as with darkening, if there is a strong edge, the feather can be very small, maybe only a few pixels. If there is no strong edge, then use a large feather, for example, **50** to **60** pixels, to blend the change more.*

Use Levels for Brightening

1. Click Enhance, click Adjust Lighting, and then select Levels.

   The Levels dialog box opens.

2. Move the middle slider to the left until the area looks properly brightened. The left and right sliders also work, but in general, the middle one looks best for this change.

Use the Dodge Tool for Small Areas

1. Select the Dodge tool (⬤). This tool lightens an area. It shares space in the toolbox with the Burn tool (⬤). Neither the Dodge or the Burn tools work well for large areas, as they tend to make the areas look blotchy.

2. Set the tool to a range that is appropriate to the tones you want to affect.

3. Use a very low exposure of 5 to 10 percent.

4. Use a soft brush sized, correctly for the area.

5. Paint over the area to lighten it in multiple strokes.

   Elements applies your changes.

CLONE EFFECTIVELY

Photos get stuff in them that do not belong with your subject. This could be as simple as dust on your sensor, which would show up as dark blobs in the sky. Or you could have a nice scene with trash in it that you did not see when you took the photograph. Or perhaps there is an extraneous hand in the photo that is distracting. You can get rid of all of these distractions by using the Cloning tool. Cloning simply copies part of a photograph from one place over another to cover a problem.

Set Up the Clone Stamp Tool

1. Select the Clone Stamp tool (⬚).

2. Select a soft-edged brush to help your cloning to blend: use the brushes with the fuzzy edges in the options toolbar.

3. From the options toolbar, select a brush size that is appropriate to the problem area you want to fix. Your cursor turns into a circle whose size represents the brush size.

Set Your Clone-From Point

4. Magnify the area that you need to clone, using the Zoom Magnifier tool (⬚).

5. Check the Aligned option in the toolbar to align the clone-from point with your actual cloning as you do the work.

6. Press the **Alt** key and click once to set a point from which the cloning tool can clone. This is the point from which it copies pixels.

Clone in Steps

7. Click to clone from the set point over your problem area.

8. Clone in steps; do not simply paint. Cloning in steps allows the cloning to blend better.

9. As you clone, change the clone-from point whenever you start seeing duplicating patterns. It is a good habit to change that point as you go.

Change Your Brush Size

10. Change your brush size as you work to make the cloning blend better with the problem areas. Use the bracket keys ([and], usually located to the right of the letter P on your keyboard) to make the brush smaller and bigger, respectively. Clone over the already cloned area using a different-sized brush if you start seeing problems.

STOP *An artefact in a photo is something that is not in the original scene or subject, but gets into the photograph because of the technology or technique used by the photographer. A cloning artifact is a repeating pattern or texture caused by cloning that pattern or texture to a new place nearby. You avoid it by changing your clone-from point and your brush size.*

WHAT LAYERS ARE ABOUT

Layers are beyond the scope of this book, but you may have noticed that they are an important part of the Elements interface. The Elements interface includes a Layer menu as well as a Layers palette. Layers are worth learning at some point because they can make a lot of adjustments faster and more efficient. This section introduces you to what they are and how they can help you. Everything shown in this chapter and Chapter 10 can be done with layers.

Layers Are Like a Stack of Photos

Photographers often get intimidated by layers. However, layers become less intimidating if you think of them as photos stacked on top of each other.

① The Layers palette shows that stack from the side and, just like a real stack, you can move layers up and down, remove them, and cut them into pieces.

Layers Isolate Adjustments

① Do whatever you want to a layer.

Ⓐ *Your changes affect nothing else in the photo.*

If you use selections with a layer, you can really isolate an adjustment so that you affect only one thing and nothing else.

Adjustment Layers Are Non-destructive

1 Adjustment layers use the controls shown in Chapter 10, but they are like filters that go over a print.

2 Adjustment layers change the look of your image.

> **A** *The original image is not altered – no pixels are damaged. You can go back and make changes as often as you want without problems. You can also experiment and delete an adjustment layer to remove a change without hurting the photo.*

Layers Work Best Step by Step

As you add layers, follow the steps that you have seen in this book, one adjustment at a time.

1 Use Levels to adjust the blacks and whites in your images.

2 Use the middle slider in Levels for midtones, as Color Curves is not an adjustment layer.

3 Use Hue/Saturation for colour.

Rename each layer by double-clicking the name and typing a descriptive name. This allows you to quickly understand what your layers are doing to the photograph.

 Layers can be saved with your image file. Use Save As to save your photo as a Photoshop (PSD) file. You can save layers to a TIFF file, but it is not a good idea because it makes the TIFF file less usable. Only Adobe products recognise layered TIFF files. If you want to save your photo as a TIFF file, flatten it first by using the Flatten Image command found in the Layer menu.

CONTENTS

12

PRINTING PHOTOS

Photographic prints have long been a great way of sharing not only your photographs, but also your experiences, your trips, your family, and so many other parts of your life. A good print is fun and a joy to have. A bad print is disappointing and sad.

This chapter gives you some ideas on how you can consistently get better prints from your photographs. Printing is a craft. This means that it takes some practice to really get good at it.

START WITH A GOOD PHOTO FOR A GOOD PRINT

Often you will hear people say that they do not have to worry about digital photography because they can fix their photos in Photoshop or Photoshop Elements. Stay away from that line of thinking! It gets you into trouble and prevents you from getting the best prints possible. Fixing images that were not shot properly from the start can be a frustrating and time-consuming process. In the end, the image is of lesser quality and is usually difficult to print.

Blurry Photos Get Noticed with Larger Prints

Sharp photos make a difference. You can get away with a slightly blurry photo if it is printed small. But if you want to print it large or crop a part of a photo and print it larger, you will really see that blur. A larger image also makes the blur larger for everyone to see.

Washed-Out Exposures Look Bad in a Print

When part of a photo is washed out from overexposure, the white of the printing paper shows through the photo. This really adds empty detail to the picture. Most of the time, it becomes a distracting part of a print, which is not something you want. Avoid this with proper exposure.

Dark Exposures Make Noise More Obvious

When you adjust a dark exposure to be brighter so that it prints well from Elements, you also reveal noise. The darker the photo, the more noise becomes obvious. This is an increasingly glaring problem as a print gets larger. Once again, avoid it with proper exposure.

Dark Exposures Cause Colour Problems

Another problem with photos that are too dark is that, as you brighten them in Elements, you can have problems with colours. The colours may lose some of their richness and tonalities and this often shows up in prints as harsh contrast, unless you spend extra time on the image in Elements.

USING A PHOTO PRINTER WITH PHOTOSHOP ELEMENTS

Today, almost all ink jet printers are capable of high-quality photo prints. However, a true photo printer can offer you the absolute best in print quality. Photo printers typically have more ink colours and finer ink dot sizes to create the best colour and tonal gradations in a print. In addition, these printers have their software and hardware optimised for the print so that photos are the star of their performance. Many photographers have two printers, a small one for printing text quickly and a larger photo printer.

Set Elements to Print

① Click File.

② Click Print.

Note: *A quick and easy keyboard command to remember for this is* Ctrl + P . *On a Mac, you use the Command key (⌘) instead of* Ctrl .

Check Your Photo Orientation and Size

The Print dialog box opens.

③ Check to see if the photo is oriented incorrectly or is the wrong size by looking at the preview.

④ Change the orientation using the buttons in the bottom-left corner.

⑤ You can make small changes in size in the Scaled Print Size area but you should go back to Elements for large changes.

Tell Elements How to Deal with Colour

6 In the Color Handling drop-down menu, choose Printer Manages Colors. With most printers, this gives you excellent results.

Some printers give better results if Elements manages colour, another option in the Color Handling drop-down menu. Then you have to choose a printer profile that matches your paper type and turn off colour management in the printer driver software.

Try a Stand-Alone Printer

A really convenient way of getting quick prints is to use a compact, stand-alone printer. You simply take your memory card out of your camera and plug it into the printer. You can have the printer print all of your photos, a selected group, or even a proof sheet showing thumbnails of all the images.

 All printers on the market today are capable of good photo prints. You may not have some of the capabilities that a true photo printer has and prints might not be quite as good, but your printer is probably capable of very good looking prints. The key is to *choose the right paper and to set the printer driver correctly. Never use non-photo paper for prints – often the glossy papers work best for standard ink jet printers.*

SET THE PRINTER DRIVER CORRECTLY

Once Elements is set to send your photo to the printer and you click **Print**, you go to your computer's operating system for printing. From there, you also access your printer's software controls, called the "printer driver". The Windows and Mac OS operating systems display the printer controls differently. Different types of printer also have different interfaces in Windows. Regardless, you have to access the interface where you can change settings, such as the paper you are using or whether you are making borderless prints.

Tell Elements to Print

① In the Elements Print dialog box, choose your print size.

② Be sure that the print resolution is between 200 and 360 ppi. If it is not, you need to go back to Elements and resize your photo by clicking Image and choosing Resize.

③ Click Print.

Open Your Printer Driver

In Windows, the Print dialog box opens and you need to follow steps 4 and 5 to get to the printer driver. (This is not necessary in Mac OS.)

④ Choose a printer.

⑤ Click Preferences to open the driver.

Set Paper Choice and Quality

This is a very important step. The printer has to know how to put ink down on the paper.

6 Choose Photo or Best Photo. You can test your results, but you will probably see little difference between these options.

7 Choose a paper in the Type drop-down menu, located in the Paper Options section.

Tell the Printer Whether to Print Borderless

The printer does not automatically print without a border, even if you make a photo that is too large for the paper.

8 See if an Advanced tab includes the Borderless command. There is always a specific setting for this option in the printer driver and you need to find and use it.

 To save ink, do not use the highest resolution your printer offers. If a print does not look good as it comes from the printer, press the Stop button on the printer. If you have problems making a print look good, print a smaller version as you make corrections. Try a test strip as described in the next section.

MAKE A GOOD PRINT

Ansel Adams had a lot to say about printing in his classic books about photography. Printing was a key part of the photo process for him. Getting a good print is really a craft. It is not simply a matter of pushing the right buttons, because ultimately the best print is still very subjective. Good printing is a skill that is honed by making prints and learning what your printer can really do, as well as discovering the quirks and nuances of your digital system.

Can You Match the Monitor?

Many people feel that if the print matches the monitor, they have a good print. There are several problems with this. First, a monitor displays colours in an entirely different way to a print. Secondly, people have quite a different psychological response to different media. Thirdly, a print must stand on its own because few viewers ever see the monitor.

Consider Your First Print a Work Print

You do need a predictable workspace so that your monitor and print look close. However, take your print away from the monitor into good light and really look at it. Could it be better? Could it be lighter or darker? Do colours need to be adjusted? Is there a colour cast? Go back to the computer and make adjustments based on this work print.

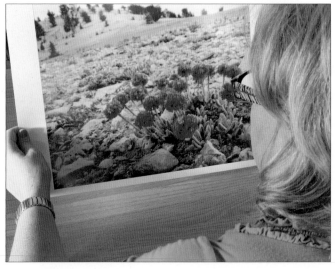

Create a Test Strip for Printing

① Use the Rectangular Marquee selection tool (▦) to select a thin strip through the important parts of your photo.

② Copy this selection by pressing `Ctrl` + `C`.

③ Click File.

④ Click New.

⑤ Click Image from Clipboard.

Ⓐ *This creates a new photo based on your selected strip. Print this test strip to save time and costs.*

Use Adjustments that You Know in Elements

Use the adjustments you have learned in Elements to improve the look of your print. It can help to write on your work print what needs to be done. Often you need to use selections to affect the colour or tone of very specific areas that look okay on the monitor but do not look good in the print.

 You might get a perfect print for your needs the first time but a work print gives you the chance to evaluate your photo as a print, not simply an automated process controlled by the computer. Ansel Adams **always made work prints, which took a long time because of the processing needed in the darkroom. But the digital photographer can try an adjustment and make a new print in minutes.**

INDEX

205